Managing
Software
Maniacs

CORIOLIS GROUP BOOKS

Managing Software Maniacs

Finding, Managing, and Rewarding a Winning Development Team

Ken Whitaker

John Wiley & Sons, Inc.

New York • Chichester • Brisbane • Toronto • Singapore

Publisher: Katherine Schowalter
Editor: Diane D. Cerra
Managing Editor: Elizabeth Austin
Editorial Production: The Coriolis Group

Designations used by companies to distinguish their products are often claimed as trademarks. In all instances where John Wiley & Sons, Inc. is aware of a claim, the product names appear in initial capital or all capital letters. Readers, however, should contact the appropriate companies for more complete information regarding trademarks and registration.

This text is printed on acid-free paper.

This publication is designed to provide accurate and authoritative information in regard to the subject matter covered. It is sold with the understanding that the publisher is not engaged in rendering legal, accounting, or other professional service. If legal advice or other expert assistance is required, the services of a competent professional person should be sought. FROM A DECLARATION OF PRINCIPLES JOINTLY ADOPTED BY A COMMITTEE OF THE AMERICAN BAR ASSOCIATION AND A COMMITTEE OF PUB-LISHERS.

Library of Congress Cataloging-in-Publication Data

Whitaker, Ken.
    Managing software maniacs : finding, managing, and rewarding a winning development team / Ken Whitaker.
        p. cm.
    Includes bibliographical references.
    ISBN 0-471-00997-0 (pb.)
    1. Computer software--Development--Management   I. Title.
QA76.76.047W478 1994
005.1'068--dc20

                            93-42456
                              CIP

Printed in the United States of America

10 9 8 7 6 5 4 3 2 1

Contents

Acknowledgments

- To my lovely wife and our cool children who have made living worthwhile.
- To those difficult, yet creative, software maniacs who have made my life so miserable and so rewarding throughout the years.

Last, but not least:

- To the mesmerizing rhythms of Peter Gabriel, Robert Fripp, Kate Bush, and Peter Hammill.
- To the beautiful South. After all of my traveling, I still haven't found a land and people more controversial and inspiring.

Ken Whitaker
Dallas, Texas

Preface

Most books on software management try to instruct readers by exhaustively describing countless theories on how to manage software projects. *Managing Software Maniacs* is different—much different. This book lays the foundation for managing modern-day software projects—using management techniques that *really work*. This book communicates issues, real case studies, and solutions that relate to on-time delivery techniques required in the fast-paced, often unstructured, field of software development.

Ten years ago, software teams were large, and projects had lots of built-in "checkpoints" and bureaucracy. Software today is developed by small teams with advanced software tools that far outpace tools available even one year ago. Yet one of the last remaining technological markets dominated by American companies (i.e., the software market) is too often poorly managed. Shocking. My intent in writing *Maniacs* has been to help you understand the software development process and learn how to lead a development organization to *success*—instead of mere *survival*.

Each chapter takes a development subject and breaks it into problem topics. For example, Chapter 2's subject is "Attracting and Keeping Developers" and one of its topics is "Rewards versus Incentives".

For each topic, I provided a problem description and then include several "Rules for the Unruly," which provide realistic guidelines for handling the topic or problem. Most topics also include "Reality Checks," which provide example situations that can help you visualize problems in a realistic context and some workable solutions. Each chapter also includes at least one "Practical Maniac Tip," which includes ideas for adapting the "Rules" to your development team.

Getting Your Priorities Straight

As we embark, I'm assuming that you are already a development manager, have aspirations of becoming a development manager, or that you are toying with the idea of someday becoming a development manager.

In this chapter, I'll cover the following topics:

- Prioritizing your customers and your business
- Exploring budgeting and capitalization basics
- Prioritizing projects (even when you want to do everything!)
- Creating a technical product strategy
- Handling difficult times

Managing Software Maniacs is designed to help you lead software development teams so that your customers and company benefit from state-of-the-art software delivery on schedule. But don't think that this book is a textbook. I've taken great care to provide unique management solutions and "from the trenches" stories to help you understand and gain control of your software creative force.

The personal computer has transformed businesses to rethink their use of antiquated, manual processing in favor of computerized solutions. The act of creating software to power these powerful "mainframes on the desk" is typically a nightmare for software companies. How in the world do you motivate your developers when company loyalty, pay, and visibility have little positive impact on their performance? And if mishandled, their performance creates a negative impact on your business.

For those readers who are not in the software development organization and who need to understand how the development mind works, this book will be indispensable.

Prioritizing the Customer

One of the traits that development personnel look for in their managers (excuse me, I mean leaders) is consistency. You could instantly lose respect if on one occasion you make decisions based on the need of the *business* and then on another occasion you make a decision based on satisfying the need of an *individual* software engineer (when everyone knows it may be the wrong decision for the company as a whole).

For this reason, I've isolated three elements that should provide guidance toward resolving critical development product issues: employee, customer, and company. Decision criteria related to these three elements tend to surface again and again.

Of course, other factors affect product decisions, such as complexity and scheduling, but the interests of employees, customers, and the company tend to dominate most decisions.

Even though we're only at the beginning of the book, it's time to take a test. Take a look at Table 1.1. Based on order of importance, which of the following sets best describes the proper priorities you should use to make product decisions? Choose either A, B, or C.

Some engineers may consider this a trick question because there are actually five additional combinations available (you know, $8=2^3$). There is no trick. The three sets shown below represent, in my opinion, the best possible options.

Need more help before deciding? I'll use column A as an example to make sure you understand how the table is organized. If you make development decisions based on company need first, then business, ethics, and policy are the "guiding lights" that drive your decisions. After prioritizing company needs first, the customer comes next. The lowest priority would be based on the employee's needs (such as the software developer). *Not a bad set of priorities.*

In determining the correct set of priorities for your organization, you must feel comfortable presenting these priorities to everyone—including business associates, customers, and employees. It would be a mistake to communicate a different set of priorities to different audiences.

For example, if you really want to be political, why not present option A to your finance organization, option B to your key customers, and option C to your developers? I know what would happen to me. I would have the wrong presentation in my briefcase and present option C to customers by mistake!

Ready for the right answer?

I have found that the choice that truly represents a customer-focused organization is option B. What? This ordering

Table 1.1 Prioritized decisions criteria

Importance	A	B	C
Most important	Company need	Customer need	Employee need
Important	Customer need	Company need	Customer need
Least important	Employee need	Employee need	Company need

should only apply to marketing or sales, right? No way! *All* organizations in your company need to focus on *the same* set of priorities.

If you don't solve customer needs first, they ain't gonna buy. If customers don't buy, then your company gets in deep financial trouble. If your business starts sinking, what pride will your employees have? Will they stay with a sinking ship? No, they really want to work for a winner. *Everyone does.*

Rules for the Unruly

Here is a set of rules that you can use to prioritize your customers and business.

Rule 1: Just because your priorities put employees at the bottom of the list doesn't mean you are anti-employee.

The first time I mentioned "customer, company, and employee" to development personnel, there was dead silence, followed by nervous whispers, mostly some variation of "What's going on?" Well, after I explained my reasons for prioritizing in this order, employees felt much less threatened. In fact, most developers thought that, in reality, my actions prioritized *employees* first!

You want that! If you make sure that your customer and company needs are prioritized as painlessly as possible, prioritizing customer first and business second becomes almost second nature.

On the other hand, you do not want this principle to be viewed as a hierarchy, where everyone knows that employees are "treated last by management!"

Rule 2: Emphasize development priorities outside of development.

Chances are that other parts of your organization (for instance, marketing, finance, operations, and sales) would be surprised that you, as a development leader, exercise decisions based on customer and business needs first.

I haven't found a single software organization that is not constantly under scrutiny for "prima donna-ism," "out of control-ism," or "out of reality-ism." These perceptions are sometimes viewed in good humor until products are not delivered on schedule. It is amazing how business principles then become important overnight.

By emphasizing consistent discipline in resolving key issues based on customer and business needs, you'll not only be a motivator to marketing and sales but also to your customers. By getting your customers to consider your development organization as a partner that has their best interests in mind, you provide a strategic sales weapon for your company. Imagine: customers then have confidence in a software supplier's management, direction, account management, and even development. Wow!

Rule 3: Practice what you preach.

In reality, very few of us practice what we preach.

So how do you know if these priorities are really taking hold in your organization? One test is to preach these priorities to your peers, to your customers (I guarantee they'll love it!), and to your developers. If they all don't echo the same philosophy, you're definitely using the wrong strategy for the wrong reasons.

If you have a difficult time getting your developers to agree to these priorities, then you have a much bigger problem brewing.

Reality Checks

Check 1: Make decisions on product features.

I had heard through the rumor mill that one of our teams was having a tough time making firm product features decisions. The team was near release of a project that had been under development for almost a year and tension was mounting.

I called a meeting with the team to address a key feature "opportunity." At this point, the opportunity was a major bug to marketing, yet an unplanned feature request to the engineers. Resolution became a question of wills.

As the meeting progressed, reasoning quickly turned into excuses and blame, and led to some unusual criteria for determining how the issue was going to be resolved.

One engineer who could solve the problem really didn't want to work on the task. His manager was in a difficult situation because he didn't want to force the engineer to resolve the problem. In fact, the engineer, at this meeting, was actually holding the team hostage because he didn't want to work on that particular problem. Would disciplinary action make sense? No. He was very talented and frankly most of the engineers had the same "disease." No decision was being made, and we had gridlock.

I decided to clear the jam by asking a question.

"Was this issue so critical that it would affect customer satisfaction if it was not properly resolved?" Interestingly enough, everyone said that it was! In fact, if it was not properly resolved, our customer support lines would definitely hear from frustrated users.

It was time for the next question.

"If this feature wasn't fixed, would there be any major financial effects to the business?" The answer came from marketing. "Two customers would probably drop maintenance contracts if this feature, which was originally promised, doesn't work correctly."

I reminded the team that by not properly resolving the issue, we risked both customer satisfaction and revenue.

The team now assumed they were being walked down a path—one that actually had an end!

Again, there was no disagreement. Marketing was happy with the results of these two questions. The questions were very non-threatening but the engineering project manager had some egg on his face in defending a position that was clearly incorrect from the customer's and the company's point of view.

So, what happened?

The issue was agreed to be resolved by the team and, even though the engineer did not enjoy working on this specific issue, there was no disagreement that he was the most skilled to complete the task. Prior decisions were frequently resolved by opting for what the engineers *wanted* to work on and not necessarily what they *needed* to work on.

This meeting served as a model from which everyone learned. Now, I obviously skipped over some key factors that would affect this decision such as risk, manpower, cost, and so on. But I've described the major issue that created the gridlock and the way the problem was resolved.

The point is this: If you don't ingrain into employees that the customer comes first and company's business comes next, you may find yourself out of business before too long. Both large and small companies are paying the price for not being customer and bottom line focused—you and your company are not exempt!

If your company enforces the "customer first and business second" priority, you can make decisions that will carry the company forward and that will win the praises of your customers and motivate your employees.

Check 2: Don't we work for the same company?

After several years of successful delivery of software products to market, our group's size (meaning our headcount, *not* our growth patterns) had grown quickly. Regular team meetings, constant communication, and attention to business and customer priorities were the rule and not the exception.

The development managers (including me) at the company's remote site were asked to help headquarters with a project that was way behind schedule. It would mean spending several months away from home but, after all, the company was in trouble.

In our opinion, the project had been grossly mismanaged and, as a direct result of the history of bad blood between the two facilities, executive management asked us to help without forcing us to help.

A meeting was called so that we could decide whether to take on the project. With a dozen managers in the room, the development director asked if we would help and "If not, why not?" Fortunately, I was the last manager called on. Otherwise, this would be a short story.

The other managers gave their reasons for not helping ("Too busy," "Family concerns," "Why help a losing cause?," and so on). And these responses came from the folks who were best suited to actually help the cause!

The project was to be performed Up North (the frozen tundra, as far as I was concerned) and would actually proceed through Christmas. Hadn't anyone explained to upper management that software developers don't work well when they're cold?

I guess not.

By the time the quest for help came to me, nobody (and I mean nobody) had agreed to help. I proceeded to explain (actually, "lecture" is a better word) to the rest of the managers why I was disappointed with them. They were better qualified in this matter, and the company had a right to ask for their help, especially in an emergency. Customers were expecting these systems, and if they couldn't be delivered on time, our fiscal year would be horrible. So I made this offer: "I will bring a kid programmer and personally help the company."

The two of us did what we were asked and spent several months away from home, helping the company and rescuing the project. There were no special incentives and no extra pay—just a desire to do what was right.

I'll never forget that decision. It has been the cornerstone for my position that doing the right thing means doing the right thing for the customer and for the business.

Check 3: It ain't my job.

In one of our department's more eventful meetings, I presented a task that needed to be performed. Although it was not an especially exciting task, it had become the highest priority need for my department. To me and my managers, this appeared to be an easy decision: Our most senior engineer needed to dedicate a couple of months to the problem at hand.

I don't remember how it happened, but at the meeting, as the task was being discussed, this particular senior engineer predicted what was going to happen next. He realized the danger of "natural selection" and, in front of everyone in the department, stated that "There is no way I'm going to work on this project even if I'm asked. It's grunt work."

Grunt work—I hadn't heard that expression in a while.

Imagine my surprise! I assured the engineer (and everyone else in the room) that although a decision hadn't been made yet on who would solve the problem, we all at times needed to help the company when asked. I reminded the folks that "Hell, about 90 percent of my job is grunt work!"

That bold statement was certainly inspirational.

After the meeting, I confronted the engineer (I mean, the prima donna). Following some moments of heavy dialogue, it was clear that he was convinced this project wasn't "his job" and that "I could get a job anywhere doing more interesting work." Well, I took him up on that and walked him out of the company that afternoon. (Note: Don't forget to tell Personnel when you do things like this.) There were other performance circumstances on his part that led me to this action, so I regarded this fast exit as a way to "put the programmer out of his misery."

Pretty vicious, right?

Maybe, but development groups tend to get to a point where they become full of themselves. To executives outside of the development organization, it almost looks like management is being held at bay by the "nerd herd." Imagine the CEO of your company being held hostage by a group of "pocket protected" vigilantes. Night after night, I replay that scene from my imaginary movie: "Revenge of the Nerd Herd." What a nightmare!

My main concern at this point was the reaction of the rest of the team. How would they take this employee's forced exit—especially since he was so talented and well liked?

To my surprise, most of the department was not only supportive of my action, but saw it as a positive reinforcement of the "customer first and business second" principle. They had been frustrated, taking lengthy assignments that they didn't particularly enjoy while this individual appeared to select only those short term tasks that interested him.

Practical Maniac Tips

Tip 1: Get everyone to practice customer first.

Rather than work with all of your development teams at once, I recommend that you work with individual teams to prove the point that it's correct to satisfy customer needs first, followed by company and then individual employees. Once your teams understand the concept, educate the organization as a whole—even the entire company.

Be a hero!

Tip 2: Test your priorities when you interview potential applicants.

Most applicants (I'd say 100 percent) will respond positively if you communicate your priorities. If, by chance, an applicant feels that the employee is more critical than the business or the customer, you may want to reconsider whether that person (your "prima donna" alert may be flashing by now) should be hired.

Development Finances

You probably have plenty of experience creating budgets and maintaining them on a monthly basis. Monthly budgeting is necessary because, without putting some fiscal planning behind your organization, you'll have no way to measure how effective you are at running your business.

However, you might not know much about capitalizing certain software development costs in accordance with Statement of Financial Accounting Standards number 86 (SFAS-86). If not, you'll need to understand this incredible benefit. If you don't really care, skip to the section *Building a Technical Strategy* later in this chapter.

What Is SFAS Number 86?

The Federal Accounting Standards Board (FASB) sets the Generally Accepted Accounting Principles (GAAP) for the Securities and Exchange Commission in the United States. This "high council" issues Statements of Financial Accounting Standards (SFAS) governing proper business accounting practices. FASB can be reached at the following address:

Financial Accounting Standards Board
401 Merrit 7
P.O. Box 5116
Norwalk, CT 06856-5116

If your finance department does not know about FASB and about SFAS-86, you've got real problems!

SFAS-86 requires your company to capitalize software development costs once technological feasibility has been established. Development costs for a product are amortized on the basis of the greater of these two criteria:

1. Each product's anticipated revenues

2. Straight line over the estimated economic life of the product, with costs charged to the cost of revenues starting with the first customer shipment of the product

Because it takes time to build technological products that will eventually bring in revenue, the ability to capitalize software development expenses helps you offset development expenses until your product is delivered. Basically, you can "shape" some of your development expenses to match your business revenue cycle.

The Major Development Delivery Phases

Take a look at a simplified delivery cycle as a set of three phases of new product delivery, as shown in Figure 1.1:

1. Study
2. Implementation
3. Maintenance

During this phase, development expenses may follow a trend of little spending at the study phase, dramatic spending during implementation, and scaled-down spending while the product is undergoing normal maintenance and updates.

In Figure 1.2, the x-axis shows development expenses over time while the y-axis has an implied dollar value ($) that indicates the cost of doing development, superimposed over the delivery cycle.

Figure 1.1 Simplified delivery cycle

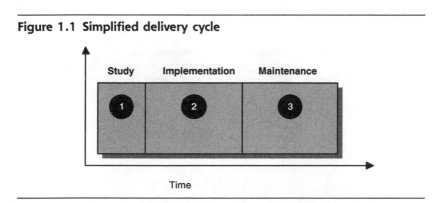

Figure 1.2 Development expenses throughout the development cycle

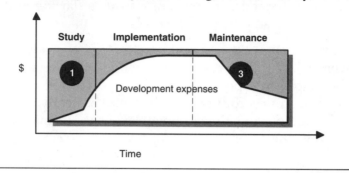

Every project won't follow this trend, but most do. So, this is the typical trend we'll continue to discuss. Sometimes the post-delivery development expenses (the maintenance part) can be dramatically smaller than those depicted in Figure 1.2. But what about revenue? Suppose I overlap a proposed revenue stream, as shown in Figure 1.3.

Prior to product release, some pre-sale revenue may take place (but don't pre-sell too far before product shipment occurs).

But what about the development expenses incurred before any revenue arrives? Rather than look at development expenses, as I've done in Figure 1.3, you should redefine the development cycle based on achieving technical feasibility and thus capitalize development expenses until the revenue truly kicks in.

Simply put, treat as expense (development costs that affect your bottom line dollar for dollar) all development costs—before

Figure 1.3 Revenue kicks in

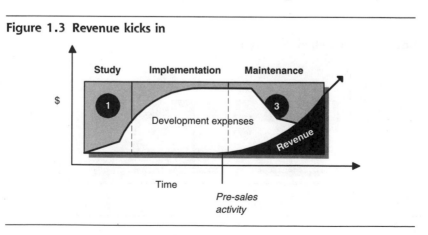

technical feasibility is achieved. The costs between technical feasibility and product delivery can then be deferred as a capitalized expense. These expenses do not affect your bottom line—they basically just represent a period of limited development expense since the IRS assumes that your company needs this "break" until revenue comes in (once you've finished the product).

This makes sense.

When revenue starts to "kick in" (in other words, *after* you've shipped the product), all of the amassed development expenses that have been deferred must now start to be taken on an amortization schedule.

When to Capitalize

Figure 1.4 shows the periods of capitalized expenses, amortized expenses (shaded), and bottom line expenses (in white).

So, how do you define technical feasibility? Although SFAS-86 has some basic requirements, your finance organization and your accounting firm need to agree on what it takes to achieve technical feasibility.

You actually defer the development costs to be taken over the lifetime of the product (as long as it brings in revenue). This requires that a financial schedule, such as a simple pro forma,

Figure 1.4 Expensing development to take advantage of capitalization

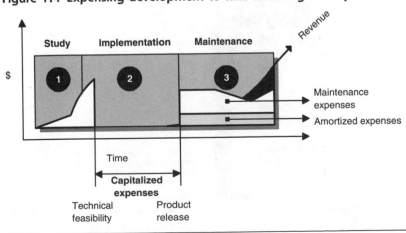

Figure 1.5 Sample product pro forma

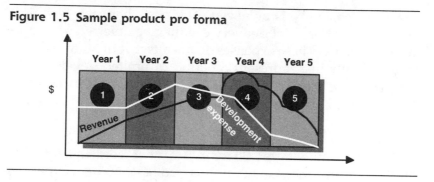

be constructed that estimates the period of recoverability and the estimated revenues. This period of time generally ranges between three to five years.

In Figure 1.5, the white line represents development expenses over time while the black line represents planned revenue over the product's lifetime. Development and marketing will need to collaborate on this pro forma to make sure the plan takes into account the effects of competition, price wars, operating system platform trends, customer buying habits, and general economic effects.

There's an even simpler way to depict whether a product will make money over its lifetime, as shown in Figure 1.6.

Figure 1.6 Planning for a product's gross profit over its lifetime

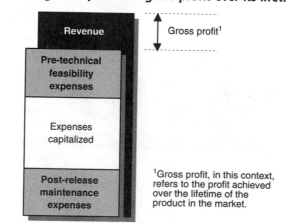

[1]Gross profit, in this context, refers to the profit achieved over the lifetime of the product in the market.

Whatever you do in evaluating a business pro forma, please do not forget the cost of marketing, training, and customer support.

Cost of Goods Sold

What about the cost of goods sold (COGs)? Believe it or not, I've seen product budgets where the cost of goods was completely forgotten in any planning. COGs generally refers to the materials associated with the production of the product for the eventual delivery to the customer.

I like to call the production department "Fulfillment" although I'm rapidly finding out that production people do not like that name.

Generally, the cost of goods includes the following materials—at a minimum:

- Documentation
- Diskettes (or whatever media you choose) and media envelope
- Box
- Registration card
- Cost of shrink wrap
- Box for shipping (make it appealing)
- Other promotional or third party offers

These items should generally be expensed as a cost to the sales department since the product volume shipped (along with the associated cost) is "offset" by the revenue brought in by sales. It is not unusual for a suggested retail price (SRP) of $199 to have a cost to dealer/distributor in the 50 percent of SRP (in this instance, $100) range. Because your company's sales organization has a profit and loss to manage, you need to consider a follow-up question: Should the $100 unit revenue have additional expenses, other than salespeople's expenses?

Yes. The COGs (usually in the $12 to $18 range for personal computer software products) should be an expense to your company's sales department. The COGs typically depends on the volume actually sold so the closer the company comes to meeting its sales estimates, the more accurate the COGs should be.

Figure 1.7 Product expenses greater than potential revenue

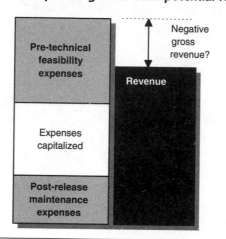

By the way, the total costs should be less than the revenue!

If you can't provide a revenue plan that demonstrates decent gross profit over the lifetime of the product, then you may need to reconsider even starting the project, as suggested in Figure 1.7.

Now, back to capitalization of software development expenses. Why even talk about capitalization? First, it is crucial that your developers understand how this works and how this affects their product's profitability. In addition, most development managers are typically "in the dark" with regard to finance and I have yet to see a reasonable, easy-to-understand explanation anywhere!

Determining Technical Feasibility

Technical feasibility should be determined by development management, with marketing and finance buy-in. Technical feasibility is reached when it is determined that the product can be built successfully to meet its feature/function goals. This could take place after a prototype is constructed or when the product fits within the desired memory (600K RAM, for example). Regardless of the specific criteria you choose to measure technical feasibility, they should be fairly consistent with all product delivery cycles.

Financing Deferred Expense

Even though you defer expenses (between technical feasibility and release), you are still paying salaries and other expenses from somewhere. In other words, product development costs take working capital. Even though some or most of your company's development expenses may be capitalized, expenses still must be paid and these payments come from assets. As a result, capitalized expenses "drain" your company's savings! Software companies that have an inordinate amount of cash (liquid assets) available can invest in development activities.

Companies that capitalize vigorously enjoy an "I'll worry about the consequences later" philosophy. Companies that have a "pay as you go" fiscal policy are generally more conservative and prefer development expenses to be treated as non-capitalized expenses. In other words, development expenses are managed much like any other expense.

The positives involved in capitalization are tremendous, but are there any negatives? You bet!

The scheduled year-on-year of revenue versus expenses (see Figure 1.5) serves as a guideline to track revenue but it also serves as the guideline that finance will need to justify capitalized expenses initially. Deferring development expenses is a benefit at the time the expense is incurred.

If a product is withdrawn from the market (many products for one reason or another don't live up to expectations), you are required to "write down" the unamortized expenses from your books. This means that, if a product is pronounced unsupported ("nuked" is a better term) and you still have a year and a half of development expenses to amortize, the entire unamortized amount must be taken as an expense at once. This can dramatically affect your company's bottom line.

Maintenance And Update Revisions

Capitalization gives your development expenses a "break" while you are creating a product that obviously has no revenue. Once revenue is obtainable, the product is normally in upgrade (or maintenance) mode. At that point, development costs should be expensed as a normal cost of doing business. If an update contains new features that are dramatic enough to bring in significant revenue over and above what normal product enhancements would bring, you may wish to consider a new amortization schedule.

Other Factors Affecting Development Budgets

Revenue per employee is a very interesting measure, and one that is becoming more of a signal of company health. Figure 1.8 shows this trend. As revenue grows over time, some companies will normally demonstrate poor revenue per employee.

When a company is in startup mode, there might be little if any revenue—it could easily take years to build a revenue base that approaches anywhere near $100,000 per employee.

For companies to be profitable, revenue per employee should be in the $150,000+ range. Some of the more outstanding software companies—such as Microsoft, Adobe, and Novell—even exceed $200,000 of revenue per employee!

For a mature software company (one that has been in business eight years or more), revenue per employee should be much greater than $100,000. If not, chances are you need some monster product "hit," potential merger, or company buyout to improve your profits.

Which employees do you count in this evaluation? *All of them:* sales, marketing, administration, and don't forget long

Figure 1.8 Revenue per employee

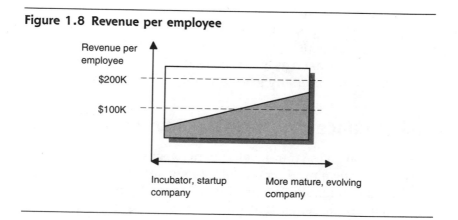

term contractors who actually perform the work of full-time employees. For the 1990s, the cost per employee in a technology company appears to be around $100,000 to $125,000. This cost includes management overhead, benefits, tax impacts, equipment depreciation, software and training, travel, office lease, communications, and so on.

Before you accept a job with a company, look at the revenue per employee trend over the past several years. Then, make sure that the company is profitable without excessive capitalization practices.

 ## Rules for the Unruly

Rule 4: Plan a sound budget.

Whatever you do, plan a budget that makes sense—as if you owned the company and had direct responsibility for its success or failure. Ask yourself some tough questions. For instance, how much money should be spent on development? A hardware company may only commit five percent of revenue to development costs. Software companies tend to commit 10 to 20 percent of revenue to software development.

In a market where product success is based on features and technical superiority, you will tend to spend a higher percentage toward software development. It is not unusual for more expenses to be allocated for product marketing rather than development, where product success is based not on features but on market presence, name recognition, and non-technical features such as "ease-of-use." This fact tends to surprise software developers.

Rule 5: Communicate how your budgets are constructed.

Your development managers are not the only ones who need to know how budgets are created. I always make it a habit to communicate to developers how our budgets have been constructed. Developers need to know why some projects have more headcount than others.

If you don't tell your developers how budgets are created, they'll probably guess the reasons (and, many times, these guesses are inaccurate).

 **Reality Checks**

Check 4: Let's just capitalize everything that breathes!

A company that dramatically undercapitalizes practices a conservative policy and is probably not taking all of the allowable benefits. On the other hand, you never have to worry about writing down huge expenses if a product does not live up to market expectations.

A company that dramatically overcapitalizes runs the risk of assuming that all of development is "free." There have been times when I had to remind my peers that capitalization implies a certain responsibility; otherwise, the consequences could be disastrous.

"What consequences?" After a product is capitalized, the amortization that is "backed up" can become enormous. Once products are released (that is, shipped to customers) and amortization starts, your development budget becomes a complicated combination of direct expenses plus staggered amortized expenses over the planned lifetime of the product (typically one to three years). Over time, the majority of your budget could actually have dramatic jumps every year—with more and more amortization expenses cranking up. (You'll need a sophisticated spreadsheet just to keep track of the multiple amortization schedules.)

Compared to the total amortized expenses, your direct, noncapitalized expenses can actually become a small part of your overall budget. *Not a pretty sight!*

Check 5: Go into markets with the intent to be the leader.

How often have you heard this one? "Put more people on the project so that we can get it out faster!" As a development manager, you know that your budget may not be able to justify the cost of additional staff. Even so, time to market is crucial, and having the right people on the right project is very important. If, on a specific platform (like DOS or Windows), your product isn't the leader in a product category or isn't even a close second, it is almost impossible to be successful in the long term. To compete against the big guns, you'll have to outperform your competition with:

- Better value
- Better promotion (bundled deals and lots of advertising)
- Better features

Even with these performance issues taken care of, assume that the leaders in your market will quickly take notice. They can usually outprice, outperform, and "out-feature" your product once they recognize your company is becoming a threat to their market dominance.

 ## Practical Maniac Tips

Tip 3: Understand your company's expense management.

You and your managers should review your company's expense standards with your financial officer. Don't be afraid to question expense techniques—chances are your financial officer will need to know how you produce software.

Make sure that your managers understand how to work with both a detailed budget and a draft budget. Since detailed budgets usually have specific line items that must be exact (such as wages and salaries, benefits, and so on), you should construct a draft budget spreadsheet that estimates the budget based on the following information:

- Average salary (with overhead and other expenses)
- A special adjustment if the developer is a contractor
- The month the developer starts work
- The project the developer will work on

The above criteria represents the basic information that can be used to quickly estimate your budget. The reason this technique works is that development's budget is dependent almost entirely on headcount costs.

Tip 4: Read your competitors' annual reports.

You can easily find out your competitor's development's percentage of expenses, level of capitalization, and the all-important revenue per employee.

An annual report can really communicate information to help you compete. You can look for:

- Level of capitalization (if there is too much taking place, they may have trouble funding new product research)
- Revenue per employee
- Debt
- Risks (most annual reports indicate risks that may adversely affect potential growth—a helpful technique to control over-zealous stockholders from expecting tremendous results)

Prioritizing Projects

The industry annals are filled with stories describing a product that initially led its category on one platform (such as DOS) but eventually lost its leadership because it was dramatically late in developing a release for a newer, more popular platform (such as Windows). This problem affects most of us in the fast-paced technology market.

The problem: How do you continue leadership on an established base while advancing to the next platform? If you are Number One on a platform, most savvy competitors will outflank you on the next platform wave (while you're still adding significant features on the current platform)! Does your competitor really lose? Not really. When customers no longer recognize you as the leader on one platform, no amount of advertising or feature enhancements can change customer buying habits on that platform.

So, how do you balance resources to maintain your leadership position when the playing field changes? Your responsibility as a development manager requires that you account for control of your resources, technology, team performance, and so on. When a product manager is frustrated because another product team seems to have more engineers, what can you do? Go over budget to satisfy the manager?

It's true that you could add more headcount, since it may be possible to capitalize more. But this is obviously dangerous if the added headcount expense does not generate incremental (that is, additional) revenue.

A better approach is to present to all product marketing and development managers a summary of the current and planned headcounts on each product. "What?" you ask incredulously. "Give up headcount control to marketing?" That *would* be a problem *if* each product manager simply voted on which development personnel were to be assigned to their projects, since development management's job is to select the right personnel for the right task.

Let the product managers negotiate among themselves which products "deserve" which headcounts, and then plan accordingly. If the results are dramatically different from any previous capitalization assumptions, you would have to resubmit these changes to your finance organization.

 ## Rules for the Unruly

Rule 6: Pass the "fiscal test."

Regardless of whether you decide to capitalize development expenses, you had better make sure that your current projects are on schedule with the fiscal plan you originally expected. This is typically a job for marketing and finance because they are better equipped to ensure that real project costs match planned costs.

Rule 7: Keep track of your employees' time on projects.

On a monthly basis, keep track of who is working on each project so that you can build a history of the actual effort it takes to deliver projects of some complexity. In addition, tracking employee time will help provide backup information in case auditors request verification of expenditures capitalized.

Reality Checks

Check 6: The headcount is all wrong!

Although marketing tries to make sure that the correct projects have the proper headcount, it is rare for product managers to be satisfied with the size of their teams. Rather than wait for the rumor mill to announce that a specific project is properly

Table 1.2 Original headcount table

Project	Current Engineers
Rainbow	5
Jason (rises from the dead)	4
Sunshine	7
Total	16

resourced, I have on many occasion preempted the situation by making headcounts visible to marketing, as I've done in Table 1.2.

Notice the project name Jason—some projects just won't die!

Although this table is highly unscientific, it will help marketing and development management prioritize which project should have the most headcount and features. Since each of the three marketing folks were dissatisfied, I provided them with an option: Help us prioritize *which* project deserves *which* headcount.

After only a few of hours of discussion, the marketing managers came up with the results shown in Table 1.3.

Without adding additional headcount, the practice of defining relative priorities helped development managers and marketing product managers assign appropriate headcounts for each product. This approach helps foster team building and enforces headcount decisions based on the benefit to customers and business.

Table 1.3 Revised headcount

Project	Current Engineers	Priority	Proposed Engineers
Rainbow	5	2	5
Jason (can't seem to kill it!)	4	1	8
Sunshine	7	3	3
Total	16		16

In other words, you need to place headcount on the projects that will most benefit customers and you need to place headcount on the projects that your business can afford.

Note: I've assumed that marketing has performed "due diligence" with their key customers and salespeople prior to a meeting like this in order to determine which product offerings have the most importance to the "real world." If headcount dramatically changes the original product business plans, product budgets and capitalization schedules may also need to be adjusted.

I personally like to perform these headcount reviews every six months or so to make sure that development and marketing's priorities are in synch. Although it is unwise to "vote" on quality assurance and documentation headcounts in this fashion, it is equally important to get guidance from product marketing on the expected quality and documentation for each project.

One warning with regard to documentation! If documentation expectations are stated only in terms of "page count," I would suggest that you buy your product marketing managers a copy of this book because these managers need further education in the proper role of documentation to a software development project.

This erroneous "page count" myth appears to be a contributing factor of the documentation group reporting to marketing, operations, or even administration. Since software engineering still suffers with the "lines of code" myth (where the quantity of source code predicts the complexity and schedule), documentation should feel right at home. Documentation absolutely deserves to be and *should be* part of development. See Chapter 4 for more information on the entire development team process.

One drawback to making headcount visible outside of development: How do you handle the people responsible for delivering the least important project? For example, how do you communicate to the Sunshine team (see Table 1.3) that only three developers, not the original seven, will be on the team?

Reducing headcount can damage the feelings of the product and development project manager—not to mention the feelings of the development team. Explaining that these are relative priorities and that a headcount review is a "snapshot" of the current situation should ease their pain. It is not uncommon for a lower prioritized project to really take off (with lots of revenue) based on its own merits and actually become, at a later time, the highest prioritized project.

Practical Maniac Tips

Tip 5: Let headcount be everyone's problem to solve.

Grab your managers, tell them your intentions, and set a meeting with marketing to review all of your projects' headcount assumptions. Taking this proactive approach will increase your visibility and mark you as a person who is not afraid to ask tough questions. Who knows, you may even find that your projects are not resourced appropriately!

Building a Technical Strategy

If your organization has a coherent, prioritized product strategy that everyone is focused on, please skip this section and proceed to the section *Handling Hard Times*.

So, you stayed put!

It's true for any business: It's not possible to provide solutions for every customer need. And if you could, your development budget would clearly be greater than the revenue you could generate. For years, I've heard statements like "We don't have a strategy." It's not that difficult to decide on an overall business strategy, but do you realize that you, in development, can actually help shape one?

Rules for the Unruly

Rule 8: Building a strategy can be as motivating as building a product.

Until I was asked to participate in a strategy planning process, I had little respect for how complicated it can be. No wonder folks in development have little regard for their company's strategic direction: They have no idea what goes into creating one.

Getting your folks involved at the right point can really help them understand how strategic direction is decided. In fact, if asked early enough, some of your folks may have some innovative ideas that you and the leadership of the company had not even considered.

On the other hand, involving your folks *every step of the way* during a strategy-building process can be disastrous. When you consider all the possible changes of direction that take place during strategy building, the ever-shifting nature of the process could very possibly become a demotivator to your folks. Getting them involved early and then near the end of the strategy-building process is a luxury that most companies can take advantage of. I guarantee that your developers will appreciate it.

Rule 9: Use consultants sparingly when creating a strategy.

It is a common technique for companies in search of identity (or strategy) to bring consultants on board. If used sparingly, consultants can easily bring a "breath of fresh air" to an organization. On the other hand, a dependence on consultants can indicate a lack of confidence in yourself or management.

Here's how to test your use of consultants: Do you use consultants for advice or for implementation? The best consultants know how to quickly assess the major issues, offer advice, and then get the hell out. If you find that you need consultants to actually *implement* their advised changes (because without them, you'll probably fail), then I'm convinced that you have either no confidence in your own leadership abilities or you have been sold quite a story from the consultants.

Rule 10: Communicate your strategy.

After you decide on a strategy that makes sense, get the word out. Whether it's through a customer road show, or with banners in your building, or with pep rallies, *just do it*. Defining a coherent strategy that everyone can get excited about is an unbelievable motivator.

In addition, take every opportunity to make reference to reinforce the strategy during meetings or other presentations.

Reality Checks

Check 7: Expand your product line.

Sometimes a company lucks into a growth business by delivering on an idea that may have come about by accident or just by providing a simple solution for a single customer that could help all customers. Before you know it, you have some success and a payroll to worry about.

However, simple product upgrades may not be enough to expand your company and allow it to grow. It is that next step in a company's history that is so difficult to lead. In some cases, the original management staff just doesn't have "what it takes" to help the company make the transition to the next stage in their growth.

Assume that you have a best-of-breed graphical drawing product that is the recognized leader in the PC drawing product category. Your company defines this business strategy: "Our goal is to be *the* provider of powerful graphical tools."

That would be a great strategy, if not for the fact that it is so wide you could drive a truck through it.

For instance, how will you know when the company has achieved this goal? How would you measure success? And, if you're not careful, you could become frustrated since this strategy touches just about every product that is released (most software products now employ some sort of graphical presentation capability). A strategy should provide the following benefits at a minimum:

1. Demonstrates a vision of the future
2. Communicates benefits to the customer
3. Is realistic and presents an intuitive or explicit path toward attainment
4. Is measurable

How about a strategy that says:

"Our goal is to provide the artistic tool of choice to complement the growing desktop publishing (DTP) user community. It is our intention to provide the most feature-rich artist tools on major operating system platforms that will become the standard of choice by the year 2000."

This is a bit more focused and makes sense to anyone listening. Your biggest hope now is that the desktop publishing market is large enough to justify this strategy. For the sake of this example, we'll assume that it is.

Assume that your product line is still fundamentally a drawing product. How do you enhance it so that it becomes the "artistic tool of choice?" And, even if you succeed in doing so, you certainly do not want to be last to market. If you agree on a plan with some rough guess of timing, I believe that marketing and development can be "joined at the hip."

Figure 1.9 shows how marketing could view its long range plan (no fancy charts—just what a user would expect from the long term goal).

Lots of backup information should accompany this simple view of the long range product strategy: competition, revenue estimates, customer testimonials, industry outlook, and so on. Figure 1.9 clearly communicates what marketing believes the user will want to see for this product to become the desktop publishing "artistic tool of choice!"

In fact, it could become the de facto standard if your company had created a "bundling" strategy. For instance, for a limited time, most desktop publishing products could be bundled with your suite of products. You could market your suite as the *DTP-Artist Assistant* (dumb name, but I like it) for an additional $50 cost to the user! Wow, who would pass this up? This could either be handled by convincing the desktop publishing software vendors

Figure 1.9 View of marketing's long range product strategy

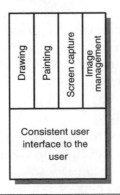

to package your products with theirs, or you could supply the vendors with mail-in cards that would give customers the opportunity to purchase your product suite for a very small fee.

Even though suite bundles tend to be "loss leaders" or make only small profits, they can dramatically increase your customer base (which is the name of the game).

So why talk about this strategy from a marketing point of view? Because it sets the tone of customer expectations first, balanced by business reality (revenue, competition, and so on).

Now, how would you technically produce a strategy that balances this marketing goal? Easy. Assume that you get this wish list from marketing:

- Product must be "best-of-breed"
- First to market is very important
- Would like a plan that gets us there in some sort of phased approach

If you're like most development managers, you'll look at your current product demands (just on your drawing product alone) and decide there is no way to develop all of the requested applications in the desired period of time. The only way t meet all of marketing's expectations would be through purchase or partnering with other products already on the market, as I've depicted in Figure 1.10.

The approach shown in Figure 1.10 takes three phases in order to meet marketing's expectations:

1. Remember that I said the company has been the industry leader with its current drawing product? Well, I forgot to mention that they have cash reserves large enough to purchase (through a combination of cash and stock) "best-of-breed" painting, screen capture, and image maintenance products already with established customer bases. So, these products could be purchased and resold as is. This purchase could be accompanied by lots of press releases to strengthen the company's position.

2. Next, a simple shell (or framework) could be created to integrate the user interface of each product. Also, minor tweaks could be made to the products so that each product could pass images (graphics) between other products in the suite.

Figure 1.10 Three steps toward strategic goals

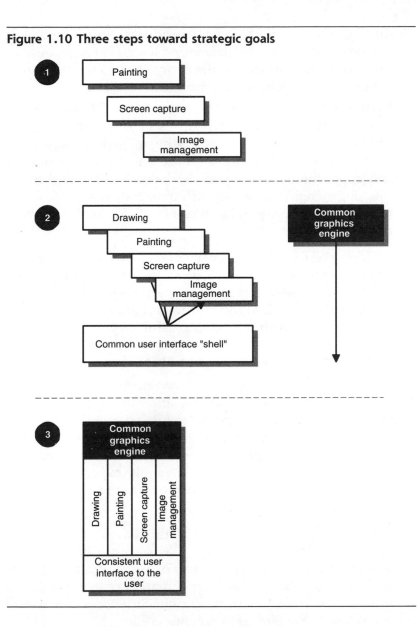

At the same time, a development project could start to construct a graphics engine that will eventually support one file format supporting each product's needs. You see, each product currently has its own unique file format and user interface. You could view this single "engine" as the brains required to handle file formats and basic drawing/painting display models for the entire product suite. In fact, this engine's applications programming interface (API) could be easily documented so that the programmers on each product team would follow *one* standard.

3. Finally, each individual product team would have to re-engineer their products to accomplish two things: Create a common user interface and access the single file system based on the engine work started in phase 2. Obviously, exporting and importing images would also be accomplished through this single engine. The user will expect each application to import and export graphic files (say, TIFF and PCX) with consistent results.

This phased technical approach may not have been elegant, but the strategy works. Marketing provides a roadmap and development implements the roadmap in a phased approach that even the marketing folks (and customers) understand and like.

This same approach can be successful for your company!

Check 8: We can't figure it out, but I bet a consultant can.

I arrived at one company where management had no strategy, the employees were disenchanted, and consultants were on board ready to help the company "get its act together."

No problem so far. After careful investigation, though, I began to notice that some fundamental issues hadn't been addressed. True, the consultants were highly experienced individuals and very talented. But much of what I saw and heard bothered me:

1. The consultants had painted a picture of a long-term strategy so glowing that everyone was seeing a bright future without much regard to the current fiscal situation. It was great to know that our untapped market potential was 200 times our current annual revenue, but current revenue wasn't even close to the budgeted revenue.

2. Development was entirely too dependent on the consultants. Prior management was so out of touch with the "troops" that these consultants acted as "go-betweens" and actually were, in my opinion, running the company. To make matters worse, employees felt more comfortable dealing with the consultant organization than with their own management.

3. Every issue was "facilitated" by the consultants. Team effort was definitely being practiced (which was great), but consensus meetings and "feel good" sessions were not resulting in clear decisions.

After about three weeks of evaluating the benefits, I felt sure that the original goals were not being achieved through the use of the consultants. So, I canned them.

What a difficult situation that was! Everyone who had come to depend on the consultants felt abandoned. The developers were now expected to work things out among themselves. ("What a drag!" they thought.) Well, I expended tremendous energy making sure that every team was properly facilitated—but by ourselves, *not* by external folks. I became personally involved with almost every confrontation, meeting, and product decision in order to demonstrate my willingness to work through issues with developers.

This is why the customer, company, and employee priorities mentioned earlier are so crucial in getting past personal egos and product team wars. Keeping consistent decision criteria helped us through a tough time. Believe me, the folks were very suspicious of me. Not only was I new to the company, but I didn't hesitate to nuke the consultants—whose job was to help *straighten out* the company.

I could characterize the software evolution in the 1980s as "getting in touch with the market and the customer." And consultants had a hey day! Lots of influential businessmen (and businesswomen) left their careers to become consultants.

In the 1990s (and beyond), I anticipate that leadership must be demonstrated from *within*, because I'm convinced that every company has tremendous talent internally. Just knowing how to bring out the best ideas and combine them into a coherent strategy is a major responsibility for software management. Strategy building must be an activity that you and your peers practice.

Practical Maniac Tips

The following ideas have been used repeatedly to successfully build strategic awareness within development organizations.

Tip 6: You should always challenge your current strategy.

Even if your strategy is "rock solid," have a one-day offsite workshop with your developers (all of them, if feasible) that will be a brainstorming session. Have someone in marketing explain the strategy to your folks. Let the rest of the day consist of idea generation sessions designed to bring out added ways to enhance the strategy or even other ideas that might be viable, even though they are contrary to the strategy.

Prioritize the best ideas and have members of your staff actually present them to marketing. This will not only improve relations between marketing and development, but will show marketing that development truly cares about the company's direction.

Tip 7: A strategy requires team "buy-in" to be successful.

You may find that your company is constantly in a "tug of war," where development needs to be involved in strategy development and marketing needs to know what development can deliver.

Why not solve the problem now? Get marketing and development management working as a team. Ask both groups to design a joint strategy that is primarily marketing based but includes development realism to provide a strong foundation. Many consultant organizations bleed companies dry because strategy-building sessions need to be heavily facilitated! Marketing and development should have the brainpower to facilitate themselves. If you really need a facilitator, use your company CEO or even the CFO!

Better yet, if you *still* feel that you need external, consulting help, plan for a strategy building session in advance with consultants. Facilitate the actual meeting yourself. Your chance of buy-in is far greater since there is a tendency to have the consulting organization not only facilitate but also to follow up with the execution of strategic action plans.

Handling Hard Times

Most companies go through "hard times" that can result from a number of external and internal circumstances:

- Downturn in the industry
- Competition adversely affecting your market share
- Change in senior company management
- Massive attrition

Although these situations sometimes can't be avoided, how you handle difficult times is critical.

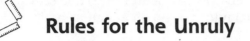 ## Rules for the Unruly

Rule 11: Forget about keeping secrets—everyone talks.

If you think developers do not talk among themselves or that rumors can be easily squelched, think again. If rumors can spread, assume that they will. If potentially negative news needs to be communicated and it does not affect company confidentiality, you should immediately make development aware of the issue.

Employees will appreciate your efforts to keep them informed. If they hear bad news from you, they'll most likely hear it in the right perspective. Rumors, from my experience, are always more negative than positive. Correcting rumors is easily twice as difficult as presenting the facts accurately the first time.

Rule 12: Don't fall victim to excessive capitalization.

Handling excessive competitive pressures may require some unplanned functional enhancements to existing products or even to the development of new products. As a result, you might be tempted to further capitalize development more aggressively than you would normally.

Unless you can justify additional capitalization with additional revenue, I would not recommend this as a realistic solution to difficult times. Some possible alternative solutions would be to:

- partner with another software supplier that has products not offered in your product line
- reduce headcount in other parts of your business to accommodate more development headcount

Rule 13: Provide your staff with month-by-month financial summaries.

Once a month, deliver to your development folks the fiscal status of the company—including revenue and expenses (actual versus target), customer buying trends, and product acceptance issues.

Developers really like to know why their product is selling well (or not selling well). During difficult times, it is critical to continue sharing financial information on a regular basis.

Rule 14: Give your development staff exposure to the finance organization.

I have never tried to shield my managers from the finance organization. It is a great learning experience for the development managers to spend time with finance to understand finance's needs in budget planning. During difficult times, developers should be encouraged to brainstorm on some innovative ideas to improve the situation. How else will your managers learn how to step into your shoes when you get promoted (or fired)?

Rule 15: Make sure you have the right headcount mix.

Who makes sure your organization has the correct headcount in each function? Don't assume that when you go into next year's planning, each organization in your company will have the proper headcount.

First, prioritize your company goals. If the company's goal is to strengthen technology offerings, then you may have the opportunity to ask for a higher percentage of headcount in development. However, if the company's goal is to strengthen customer account management and it is felt that the product offering is pretty solid, perhaps development staff should be a smaller percentage and the sales organization should enjoy a higher headcount. Ultimately, the company's finance officer or CEO will have to make this determination because I've rarely seen any executive "volunteer" to have less headcount in his or her organization to satisfy the company's common good.

Practical Maniac Tips

Tip 8: Take the responsibility and plan for the right headcount.

Rather than wait to be asked to plan for next year's budget, have each of your managers create a table (or spreadsheet) with this simple information:

1. Headcount per month
2. Duration of product schedule
3. Major risks

This spreadsheet should be smart enough to calculate the total cost of a project (you should have an average salary per discipline in development) and total man-months each project requires. In addition, if your spreadsheet is really smart, it could calculate the cost breakdown of each discipline (by discipline, I mean engineering, quality assurance, documentation, customer support, and so on). In addition, you could easily calculate the percentage (in terms of cost or headcount) that each discipline takes for a given project.

As you review this analysis, you should quickly verify that projects are properly resourced. You can use these spreadsheets to review headcounts with product marketing for next year's product planning. By using this planning technique (instead of hopping directly into detailed budget worksheets), you'll save a lot of time and aggravation.

During difficult times, nuke those products not living up to their revenue potential. Now is the *wrong* time to become sentimental!

In Summary

Prioritize toward customer first, business second, and employees third.

If you don't, I guarantee your business will suffer.

Practice realistic, conservative budget planning.

An analogy could be made to your own finances. Spend based on what you earn. If you must borrow, then do so with a plan on how you can pay the funds back. This philosophy applies to capitalizing software development expenses.

Build a technical strategy.

Even if your company has a weak marketing strategy (most companies suffer from this), that's no excuse to let your development teams suffer without their own plan. Development needs a technical roadmap: Provide one for them with your team's help.

Use consultants sparingly.

Using consultants for short-term contracts or seminars can help *you* to recognize and solve key issues. *Depending* on consultants for long-term contracts can only achieve one thing: Dependence on *them* to recognize and solve key issues.

Have the right headcount.

To prepare for downturns in your market, don't hire beyond a reasonable goal. I would much rather operate "lean and mean" than risk a layoff. If a layoff takes place, it is a humiliating experience for the employees and, to a large extent, the blame rests on management for not properly watching the business. (And by management, I definitely include *me*.) Each project should have the proper headcount based on strategic need or current revenue projections. It's that simple.

Attracting and Keeping Developers

The title of this book is loaded with meaning. I used a variation of it several years ago in a want-ad header designed to attract "killer" developers. And did it work!

In this chapter, I'll discuss the following topics:

- Keeping developers happy with rewards or incentives
- Why keeping employees is more difficult than recruiting them
- Successful hiring techniques used by the masters (well, by *me*)
- Performing career planning and employee surveys

Rewards versus Incentives

How many times have you heard these two lines from upper management or marketing?

"Couldn't we get the software project out faster if your folks put in more hours?"

"We are depending so much on this product. Let's dangle cash to motivate the engineers *if* they deliver products by March!"

Motivating developers is a difficult skill to master—and motivational success depends on your company's culture.

If your company is very aggressive and has little regard for ethics (one company comes to mind) and the goal is to get products out at all costs, then by all means offer cash incentives!

But be prepared to pay the consequences.

Most of us are in this business because of the technical challenge. This fact applies to writers, testers, and software engineers. But we also have to make a living. So, it is rare for anyone to leave a company for more technical challenge and less money. (An exception may be to a startup company where the long-term financial opportunities are potentially stupendous.)

Consider what motivates other organizations in your company. Salespeople are motivated by closing the sale, attaining quotas, being recognized, and making more money. Marketing is similar: If the products they are managing are successful, the company will grow (and so will their wallets or purses).

If your company has anything to do with software development (which is why you're reading this book, right?), your chief financial officer's (CFO) motivation should be to deliver *anything* to the market in order to save face with the stockholders and board of directors, and to protect his or her bank account. There is nothing wrong with these motivations because it makes sense to desire success and all its financial rewards, right? Of course.

So what's wrong with this picture?

The software folks (those "maniacs" upstairs) don't seem to care. They wear T-shirts with strange slogans, and appear to be motivated only by pizza! How in the world do you motivate them to get products out faster?

Deciding whether to use rewards or incentives is a key management challenge that most software organizations have to face. I find that this issue comes up about once every six months—*like clockwork!* In fact, every time I give a *Managing Software Maniacs* presentation and this topic comes up, there are several folks in the audience who can't wait to tell their incentive horror stories.

Rules for the Unruly

I've found that, no matter where software developers reside (Dallas, Research Triangle Park, Boston, San Jose, Chicago, or elsewhere), some basic rules apply regarding rewards and incentives for developers.

Rule 16: Reward, never incent.

Developers need to be rewarded after they have accomplished goals. Although a project has many goals (or milestones), there is nothing like delivering a quality product that satisfies market needs especially on or ahead of schedule. I hope the example situations in this chapter demonstrate just what can occur if you, as a manager, fall victim to incentives.

Rule 17: Motivate developers, not just engineers.

Your organization includes several disciplines: engineering, documentation, quality assurance, and so on. Your group might even include support personnel. If you depend on teamwork to deliver products, the best way to kill teamwork is by rewarding only a portion of the team (for example, just the engineers).

Rule 18: All products are important.

Some products are more critical to the bottom line of your company. However, if you reward only those developers who work on "high profile" products, they won't be motivated to associate themselves with smaller or less glamorous projects. I've fallen victim to this myself and will never do so again.

Rule 19: Openly communicate the reward system.

This is a tough one. Maybe you should just keep your reward plans quiet, right? Well, would you rather have the company's reward system communicated via the rumor mill? If you have a reward system, let Personnel help you openly communicate the opportunity for rewards.

Rule 20: Reward through private recognition.

It is very satisfying for a manager to hand-deliver a private check (say, $1,000) to a developer for exceptional performance. When I've discussed whether public or private awards should be given, 100 percent of development management (and developers themselves) continue to reenforce that developer awards should be *private*.

But isn't it strange that, in other organizations outside of development, public recognition is desired? Teamwork is a mystical force that you, as a development manager, should respect. Public rewards will alienate the recipient! If you don't believe me, just try it once.

A $50 gift certificate doesn't work either. Cash allows the employee to use the money in his or her own way. Surprisingly, some of your developers will use the money to buy some software or hardware for their own home use if their work is also their hobby.

Rule 21: Reward timing is critical.

Don't wait a couple of months after a major accomplishment before you reward someone. Reward immediately after exceptional performance. An official letter from you and senior management addressed to the recipient can really mean a lot. And one way to reduce project risk is to reward key developers early in a product cycle (for example, at the alpha milestone).

 **Reality Checks**

Check 9: A famous software provider does Hawaii.

Not too long ago, a famous software company announced that, in order to deliver a specific product (already one year late), a vacation in Hawaii would be awarded to the developers as a high-profile incentive.

What was the catch? Well, the product was to be delivered by a specific date. Were people excited? You bet! Lots of long hours and effort went into the much-publicized project. In fact, spouses were already planning their Hawaiian-travel wardrobes.

As the weeks became months, the desired delivery date came and went. The software product was *not* completed on schedule. What was senior management to do? What would you do if you were the manager? There seemed to be a major flaw in management's expectations: *wanting* a schedule to occur appeared to be different from gaining cooperation to meet a realistic schedule. During the early days of the Hawaii excitement, "reality" was noticeably absent from everyone's vocabulary.

So, it's not surprising that the date was missed—and missed by a wide margin. The Hawaii trip did take place many months later but only for a select few. And were the developers happy about the experience? Not at all: They felt a bit *used*.

Now take a look at a case that's even worse.

Check 10: You deliver by June, you'll get $Big Bucks$.

Another major software player decided to "dangle" incentive money in front of its developers to get an already late product out the door on a very aggressive schedule. In the heyday of the early software pioneers, the high-growth companies had no problem with throwing around lots of cash. When you sell software for $300 and the cost of goods (COGs) is roughly $15, you have a lot of room to play with! (I know there is a lot of research and development money that you need to consider, but how many industries have the level of profit margins that the software industry currently enjoys?)

Anyway, senior management was so fed up with the development process and the fact that dates were constantly being missed that they decided to try a new tactic: money. The company's once-solid market penetration was eroding rapidly.

New competitors had been releasing products, and these up-starts were beginning to chip away at the product's market share. And once a product's market share begins to erode, very few companies are able to recover.

The developers were gathered together to hear the proclamation from management:

"If you deliver project X by this date, you will each receive cash based on both your contribution and your salary. Some of you stand to become very well off financially."

Wow—some message! The developers were getting excited, management was immediately realigned, and the entire company was in a frenzy. Bonsai! Food, cots, and faster PCs were purchased to get "everyone in the mood." Personal credit cards were already reaching new limits since this loot was a "done deal." This wasn't a fight—it was *war*.

Days became weeks, weeks became months. Progress was being made, but some hasty decisions had required some key module rewriting. The thinking in development was, "Oops! A *little* setback, but we can recover. Remember, we're gonna get rich!"

The dictated delivery date came and went and no product had been delivered, although the developers were close. (Surely you've heard about the infamous "I'm Close" project milestone?) Senior management gathered the developers together and said, "Okay, we understand the original date was a little too unrealistic; the offer still stands, but release by November."

By this time, though, developers were losing the stamina required to continue the necessary long hours and, to nobody's surprise, teamwork (a key developer motivator) was going out the window.

The second deadline wasn't met either and two events happened:

1. Developers were losing confidence in themselves and with the company that wanted unrealistic product delivery and endless personal time commitments.

2. Management was angry because they had provided every possible luxury to development in order for them to simply deliver "a product."

The rest is history.

Senior management withdrew the incentive and threatened jobs since developers were employed to deliver even without the need for extra compensation. Some of the software engineers (the good ones) left the company, morale was horrible, and by the time a product was delivered, the company's market share had eroded.

What a terrible lesson to learn.

To make matters worse, the product quality and design were so poor that, due to the frenzy to deliver, corners were cut throughout the project. The product could hardly support future enhancements.

There's more. Read on . . . .

Check 11: Why not reward just the leader, not the team?

This one is my personal favorite because I got burned myself.

In order to deliver a critical product, one of my managers was promised a huge bonus by another member of the executive staff if his team delivered a product to market by a specific date. I was new at the company, and even though I disagreed with the incentive, I had to honor the commitment.

The project (and the team) went through hell, but luckily delivered the product on schedule (well, actually a couple of weeks late, but that ain't bad). About a week after delivery, the manager demanded the incentive he had been promised. And we delivered it to him (less taxes, which—this shouldn't surprise you—he didn't like!).

The rest of the team's so-called bonus? There wasn't one.

Not only was his team upset with him (and the company), many basic engineering fundamentals were ignored in order to make the delivery date and we had to deliver a major bug update just one month later! To top it off, the manager quit the company two months later.

Man, oh man! That sure was a fun time. *Not.*

 Practical Maniac Tips

Tip 9: Construct a reward system that makes sense.

As I discussed earlier, it is critical that you design a reward program that matches your company's culture and needs. I use the word "culture" loosely to indicate the values you place on development, *not* as a force to be reckoned with.

As an exercise, I recommend that you construct a workshop specifically aimed at resolving reward factors within your development organization. (Use other personnel or outside facilitators if you feel a little uncomfortable with the subject.)

I suggest the following steps:

1. Talk specifically to management and the personnel department to make sure they will endorse administration of a reward system and to get their input before proceeding.

2. Meet with your development management and indicate your willingness and need to provide some firm financial motivation opportunities. Ask for volunteers in each development discipline to form a task team. You may choose at this point to include or to exclude the personnel department. (My vote is to exclude them for now.)

3. Meet with development management and the task team to address goals, options, and the type of techniques that can be agreed upon. Have one of the task team members (or your management) draft the minutes and a recommendation.

4. Now, assume that you've presented recommendations for endorsement to upper management and the personnel department (I told you they'd get back in the picture), and assuming that you've gained approval, you then present it to development. I would not post the recommendation because it provides daily reminders of potential rewards, thus setting inaccurate expectations. If you did not gain approval, go back to step 3.

5. Deliver, reward, and motivate. You'll be amazed at the results.

Questions and Answers

The following questions always seem to come up at my maniac seminars, so I think I should answer them here.

Q: How much should I reward?

A: Well, that depends on your budget constraints. Too *little* is humiliating. Too *much* could set future wild expectations. Any rewards should be privately agreed upon by *all* of your management staff since developers do talk and rumors of "So-and-so got $500" could cause problems—especially if your management staff did not agree beforehand.

Q: Does it make sense for one person to receive several rewards?

A: Yes, it makes sense. Chances are that the person is absolutely exceptional. That's what rewards are for! Rewards provide a delivery of the "pay for performance" philosophy so common in today's technology companies.

Q: How about team rewards?

A: Sure. Reward the whole team with a shipping party. Release parties provide a good way for the team to let off steam and are a lot of fun. Gag awards, *drinking*, dancing, *drinking*, pool, *drinking*—these are just what most development teams need to unwind. (You know you've had a successful party when one of the men leaves the party with the wrong coat—a woman's coat! No joke: it really happened.)

For the past six years, I've asked the entire team to autograph "User's Manual" covers, which are then nicely framed and given to everyone who participated (including any and all contractors). This reward-party event strengthens the team's morale and leaves folks with a memento directly related to the project. Project keepsakes don't have to cost a lot.

Using Want-Ads Effectively

I am constantly surprised at how boring want-ads are, even though companies are trying to attract key people. Have you ever wondered why so many respondents don't meet your requirements? Consider this exchange between a hiring development manager and the VP of development:

"How many resumes did you get?"

"Well, we got about 100 resumes, but *only* about five are worth investigating."

"You've got to be kidding?"

Sound familiar? It almost seems a waste of time and energy to use the newspaper as a hiring medium. In fact, I hear from prospective hires that they rarely find decent jobs when they respond to classified advertisements.

However, if you use the appropriate medium correctly, advertisements can be very effective.

Rules for the Unruly

Rule 22: Advertise as though you want to hire yourself.

Your advertisements need to show the level of enthusiasm that would drive even *you* to respond. Leave the boring advertisements to your competitors!

Rule 23: Pre-screen applicants with the ad.

If you don't put enough detail into your advertisement to screen out unqualified job seekers, you'll get tons of resumes that don't represent the type of individual you thought you were advertising for.

There are some other wild ways to get the word out.

Have you ever thought of using a billboard that people can read on their drive home? Afternoon rush hour is a good time to catch disgruntled prospects who are tired and upset by the bad day they had on the job. Semiconductor firms have used that technique for years.

Reality Checks

Check 12: Don't hire your own employee.

Consider a company that has placed a "blind ad" (without the company name) in order to get the best talent available without indicating that they were hiring. Management's thinking seems to be: Our company's name doesn't communicate the caliber of folks we need to attract.

Another reason to place a blind ad is to keep a low profile due to the potential for wrong interpretation of advertisements by competitors or even internal employees.

This particular classified ad listed the virtues of the company: salary, career path, sound company direction, and so on.

The ad attracted lots of good resumes. In particular, one of the most promising resumes had been submitted by one of their own employees! It appeared to the employee that his company did not offer decent salaries or company direction and the advertisement really communicated the values a company should have.

What a disaster: employees responding to their own company's advertisement!

Check 13: You don't have to recruit in the paper.

A CEO friend of mine leads (notice I said "leads," not "manages") a growing software company. He was tired of spending money on recruiters and expensive ads, so he put himself into a programmer's head. "What would interest me? "

His premise was that the really *great* programmers are not looking for another job.

Well, he realized that most creative engineers would attend a certain event in town, so he rented some inexpensive airplane time (less than $200) to fly a banner around town stating that "We're hiring creative programmers. Phone 555-8392."

The local press was so interested in this stunt that they interviewed the president on the evening news that night! For less than $500, he got an incredible level of exposure, while most advertisements cost much more!

Check 14: Advertise with the intent to get maniacs.

We were looking for high-end graphics engineers and testers, and we knew how hard they were to find (the good ones, that is). One of my managers said, "What we need are maniacs like us."

That's the answer, I thought.

We wrote an advertisement that hit multiple nerves:

```
WANTED PC SOFTWARE MANIACS

So, you want to be a software "star"? Well, have we got the
right place for you! If you possess the following skills,
please read on:

• C++ and C programming skills
• Windows graphics programming (>2+ yrs)
• BS in mathematics

If you do not possess the following traits, do not bother to
contact us:

• Ability to work on a team and take constructive criticism
• Ability to work with minimal specifications
• Ability to deliver projects on time

Contact the following address for more information.
```

Although you may think this advertisement is a little rude, we received incredible responses. One applicant was so excited that in his cover letter he said, "Your ad really communicated to me that you are exactly the type of company I'd like to work for." Unfortunately, in his haste to rush us the letter, he forgot to include his return address and his resume!

We received negative responses, too. One applicant wrote our president and complained that "The advertisement for software maniacs represented an organization out of touch with reality."

He went on: "There was little mention of detailed specifications, process, or proper business protocol that I feel was missing. I am not applying for the demeaning job you posted; instead, I'm applying for your vice president's job, since I think he's nuts."

He was not invited for an interview.

Practical Maniac Tips

Tip 10: Improve your recruiting want ads.

For a team-building exercise, I would recommend that you spend a little time with your managers emphasizing advertising.

1. Here's the best way to get your managers excited about advertisement issues: Have them spend a few hours with you going over goals, agreements on how to qualify applicants in the ad, format, and other ad issues.

2. Once each month, gather your hiring managers together and review competitors' want ads. The purpose? To make sure that you know what your competitors are looking for and to further improve your own advertisements' effectiveness.

If you find that your advertisements bring in too many of the wrong resumes, change your ad. Most people interested in keeping current in their careers will periodically scan the Sunday classifieds. You want to provide something that will communicate with prospects in a period of a few seconds.

Can You Hire Effectively?

What a dumb topic, right? Wrong. How many mistakes can you make trying to hire? Let me count the ways! Anyway, let's list the basic steps required to successfully hire:

1. Place an advertisement
2. Interview
3. Hire

Seems easy. A few hours of your time, right?

In fact, some development organizations are in such a hiring frenzy (whether due to growth or attrition, it doesn't matter) that management finds itself spending a majority of its time doing nothing but interviewing and checking references. During work, at night, on weekends—whew! Is this effort really necessary?

The rewards of bringing in top-notch talent make it all worthwhile. But rarely do we schedule enough time away from our normal duties to accommodate the countless hours it takes to hire someone.

Rules for the Unruly

Rule 24: Advertise as if you were hiring yourself.

Although this appears to be obvious, it's an often neglected rule. So, I've devoted an entire topic to this earlier in the chapter.

Rule 25: Interview in one session if you can.

When you bring in an applicant, the results could be one of the following:

1. The applicant appears to be qualified, but additional rounds of interviews need to take place.
2. The applicant is not right for the job, so the prospect is escorted out (sometimes before the interview is completed).
3. The applicant is perfect and, assuming no serious problems during reference checks, should be hired immediately.

Which result do you prefer?

Obviously, the third scenario is the best of all worlds. If you follow many of the guidelines addressed here, it's likely that you will find the third scenario occurring more often!

Rule 26: Interview with a good cross section of the team.

Failure to interview without all representatives of the team organization taking their turn (*not* interviewing each candidate as a group) will result in automatic follow-up interviews. Just because you are interviewing a software engineer does not mean you shouldn't involve other key team members (such as quality assurance, documentation, support, and even marketing). I have uncovered many team-related issues using this "team interviewing" technique.

I insist on this technique and it really does make a difference.

Rule 27: Don't do group interviews.

Once I found out that all members of a team performed an interview within two hours and I asked how this was possible. "Well," replied the exuberant project manager, "we interviewed the applicant together—all at once!" Although the intentions were correct, I was actually able to ask the applicant what he thought about the process. He told me he did not enjoy being put under fire while surrounded by four to five engineers.

Don't do it. It's humiliating and, quite frankly, intimidating.

Rule 28: Prepare and rehearse beforehand.

Do you realize the merit or necessity of each question you ask during an interview? By checking with an applicant, we found that about 50 percent of each interviewer's questions and comments were *identical*. What a waste of time for everybody involved!

Before you start interviewing, it makes sense to prepare. By making sure that each interviewer is not replicating the same information, you can make sure that each team member focuses on specific job issues. Also, I find that a quality hour on the phone with a prospect is needed to determine the potential for an interview. If you like the resume and your only communication with the individual is through a resumé, chances are that the applicant may be less qualified than you suspect. Anyone can write an amazing resume.

Rule 29: Set honest and realistic expectations.

If you find yourself stating only the positive aspects of the job, you are actually doing a disservice to the applicant. You need to present both the positive and negative issues, as objectively as possible. No job opportunity is perfect—otherwise, software developers would never leave their company. Most companies cannot keep a software developer more than 18 months before he or she moves on. (And you thought this was the perfect job!)

Can't think of any negatives for your company?

Boy, I can! How about benefits, dress code, stress, inconsistent marketing strategy, frustration with quality, and on and on? If you don't set proper expectations, the new hire will figure out that things aren't all that rosy about a month after being on the job. And never tell the applicant during the interview that he or she "appears to be qualified."

Rule 30: Stay away from personal issues.

At times, you may try an "ice breaker" by talking about an applicant's hobbies or family members. Don't do it! Always consult your human resources representative if you need guidance on this subject.

Rule 31: Follow up quickly with applicants.

Whatever decision you make with an applicant, please follow through with either a "no thank you" or "we're going to check references" within a week after the interview. If you fail to do so, the best applicants might decide to look elsewhere or might give up on your company.

 **Reality Checks**

Check 15: I am really interested in your hobby.

An applicant had some very interesting hobbies on his resume: Biking, various civic organizations, church, guitar.

(Have you ever noticed that everyone plays the guitar?)

Well, the interviewer was very interested in the various civic organizations and pressed for more personal information, even though it was not related to the job:

"Just some local, in-town organizations."
"I belong to the Kiwanis. What is it—the Elks?"
"Oh, I'd rather not say."

"Oh, come on. We live near each other, I'd like to know."

"Okay, it's the Ku Klux Klan. I've been a member for 5 years now."

Oops.

The interview from that point on became a little tense and although the applicant did not get the job for technical reasons, the applicant always considered that he was passed up due to his personal affiliations. The potential for lawsuit in a situation like this is very real. You could be playing the role of evaluator of not only an applicant's skills, but also of his or her unrelated activities. Your personnel organization can probably help you understand what to say and what not to say.

 ## Practical Maniac Tips

Tip 11: Lead your own interviewing workshop.

I have found that few workshop ideas are effective regarding effective interviewing.

1. Gather your managers together and construct a hiring workshop in order to improve the effectiveness of the dialogue. Do a "role play," with hiring managers taking turns as the interviewer and as the applicant. It can be rather humorous but, all in all, this is a great team-building exercise.

2. Test how good the interview process is by checking back with those whom you didn't hire. The applicants you end up hiring aren't going to give you negative constructive criticism (at least not until they get jaded after several months on the job).

3. Work with the personnel department in order to verify that your techniques are following company personnel and ethics guidelines. It is a good idea to periodically meet with the personnel department and your managers to review interviewing fundamentals.

    How you present yourself during the interview process could actually help attract other folks through word of mouth. The bottom line is that the personnel department should coordinate hiring workshops that will help your managers understand hiring fundamentals.

Try to stay away from the $99 generic interview workshops that are presented at most cities (not unlike the traveling circus). They are too "watered down" and are not nearly as effective as building interviewing techniques with your hiring managers and interviewers.

Dealing with Recruiters

I've had such difficult dealings with recruiters that I put together a presentation called "Why I Hate Slime Headhunters." This presentation was actually given at an annual professional recruiter seminar. (I won't mention where this took place to protect the innocent.)

The presentation was humorous, as you can gather from the title. It had to be: the seminar was full of recruiters. Why were they interested in hearing from me? Because a lot of us hiring managers have had so many bad experiences with recruiter techniques that, rather than working with good recruiters (and there are a few!), most of us avoid them.

Rules for the Unruly

Rule 32: Select a recruiter you can count on.

Do not work with any recruiter that calls you too many times (to the point of being a pest), or you will be inundated with resumes. I've seen situations where the same applicant has been represented by multiple recruiters!

If the recruiter doesn't offer some sort of screening process or doesn't even meet the applicant, I send them packing. If you find that the applicants you interview based on a recruiter's recommendation are not qualified, avoid using the recruiter. The recruiter simply doesn't understand what you need.

Rule 33: Negotiate fees that benefit you.

Recruiters have a wide range of fees they can charge, but most recruiters require placement fees in the 30 to 35 percent (of total yearly salary or regular wages) range. They will, under certain volume agreements, agree to fees as low as 20 percent. These volume agreements require that you commit to hire a certain number of applicants in a given year. Don't agree to this if you don't have to! I continue to negotiate fees in the 20 percent range without signing anything.

Reality Checks

Check 16: Watch for unethical behavior.

Once, we used a great recruiter to hire a senior engineer and were very happy with the hire. About six months later, a rumor circulated that the same recruiter was calling in to the new hire, not to the hiring manager. He was trying to "outplace" the same guy he had sent to us six months ago.

I invited the recruiter to my office to talk about upcoming hiring.

Or so he thought. Instead, I informed him that I knew what he was doing and not only did I not appreciate it but we would never deal with him again. He denied any wrongdoing but I've never regretted the action and we never heard from him again.

Check 17: Use on-site recruiting.

My best experience with a recruiter occurred when I hired a recruiter on-site. We interviewed recruiters (boy, was that weird) and selected one. He met with our managers and set up shop on-site. He ran the want ads, "scoped" competitors, phone-screened applicants, and handed us prioritized resumes that he considered to be stellar.

If you haven't considered on-site recruiting, you may be missing a spectacular opportunity.

Practical Maniac Tips

Tip 12: Deal with recruiters correctly.

Dealing with recruiters is often a very difficult task. If you must deal with them, here are some suggestions:

1. Up front, negotiate a rate based on the number of hires you expect to be made. Even if the going rate is 30 percent, don't be surprised if you can't negotiate a rate of, say, 20 percent.

Impossible, you say? I've done it several times. And without even a commitment of specific headcount—just *intentions*.

2. As a follow up, have your best recruiters (you know, those with the most greasy hair) come in to discuss needs with you and your hiring management staff. It really helps when everyone involved with hiring (your managers and a few select recruiters) is in agreement with your expectations.

Career Planning

This topic is my favorite. But what is career planning, really? Development managers are not doing their job if I can't ask any employee about his or her career path without getting an immediate and realistic response. Try it. I bet 95 percent of your developers cannot respond to a request for them to recite their career path.

So what do I mean by "career path?" I mean the steps a person needs to take to achieve his or her long-term career goal. If a person responds to my question with "I haven't really thought about it—my next step is to finish this DLL module," then he or she is *not* planning. Developers tend to be apathetic and they really just want to be technically challenged. However, when they are standing in front of you with their resignation letter and saying they are leaving "for a better opportunity," someone in another company has done a better job of career planning than you did! There are exceptions, of course, where things just do not work out. But, in general, we've all witnessed this situation too often.

I expect managers to develop successful projects and successful people.

Rules for the Unruly

Rule 34: Career planning is more important than a merit increase.

It is not unusual for performance and career planning discussions that formerly took place once a year to be combined with merit increase discussions.

You should "de-couple" career planning feedback from regular merit-increase discussions. Why? Career planning should be a relaxed, two-way discussion.

I like the idea of communicating performance feedback in relation to career planning since the employee really would like to know where his or her career is going based on their performance to date.

Rule 35: Test that your managers are truly communicating career planning.

You should be able to ask developers what career goals are and what they think they need to do to accomplish these goals. Many times, it is difficult for an employee to feel comfortable responding, so you may have to "work it" a little. For example, rather than ask, " What is your career path?" you could try the following ice-breaker:

"I've been really impressed with your performance on project Jason (you know, the project that rises from the dead). Your manager has shared with me your performance this past period. You know that we have both technical and managerial career ladders, right? Do you believe that you and your manager have talked through what makes sense for you?"

The words "career path" didn't even come up!

Suppose the developer replies this way:

"I plan on taking one more leadership course and after this project I hope to be a team leader. My goal is to have your job one day but I know I'm not ready yet."

That response is the result of career planning!

Reality Checks

Check 18: Career-plan at least once a year.

At least once a year, I sit down with each of my direct reports to review performance and how I believe the employee is advancing toward his or her career opportunity.

Many times I hear something like this from developers:

"I'm not sure where my career is going at this company. My boss rarely gives me any feedback."

Unfortunately, career-path feedback can be interpreted as more negative than positive. Career-path feedback should be designed to be constructive—never demeaning or spiteful. I have seen few career-planning documents by other development organizations, but I have seen performance appraisals that start out with a phrase like:

"You are a failure as a development manager."

Wow, good introduction! With openings like this, you can forget about getting decent career planning from this jerk of a manager.

Practical Maniac Tips

Tip 13: Develop career path mentality.

If you can find a great seminar that trains managers in career planning fundamentals, sign yourself up (along with your managers). If there is no such seminar, develop one yourself! All it takes is common sense.

As you attend or give these workshop exercises with your managers, consider the kind of career path information you would want for yourself.

Tip 14: Construct a career path document that clearly communicates your feedback.

Put together a document that clearly communicates what you think your employee's strengths and weaknesses are. This could include such information as:

- Number of years on the job, along with job title
- Strengths followed by weaknesses
- What you perceive is the next position for the individual
- A summary of those attributes that you expect for this next position
- Steps that the individual needs to take before being considered for the next position

The sample career planning document on the next page should help you visualize a career path review that I did for one of my managers. (The name was changed to protect the innocent.)

1994 Development Goals

- Deliver quality, global products based on market demands on or ahead of schedule
- Establish processes to effectively manage our business
- Hire and career-coach first level project management staff

My only purpose in this communication is to coach you to enhance your strengths.

Manager Mike's performance is as follows:

Strengths

1. Outstanding problem solving skills
2. Superb technical and SQA skills
3. Within group, communication skills are good and getting far better (his people always know what is going on)—he has developed trust with his teams
4. Speaks his mind, represents his folks well (gained tremendous respect outside of development troops!); Mike is simply a "breath of fresh air"
5. Takes constructive feedback extremely well and is developing into quite a coach for his team members

Weaknesses

1. Under stress, Mike will appear to "have his mind made up" (example: common architecture)
2. "Buy-in" sometimes falls by the wayside when decisions have to be made (Mike has made significant progress here, but the potential to "slip back" is there)
3. True experience running a $30M development business—we may all learn the hard way—i.e., how to get creative results out of people (Project Jethro delivery, proposals "nailed" on time)
4. Organization and time management skill (Mike struggles to keep his calendar open & "how can I get my job done with all of these meetings?...")
5. Vision and strategy skill building is lacking and needs to be "energized" (Mike is more tactical than strategic)

Priorities To Grow

Mike is now really in-charge of a business that was mine only six months ago. He has been promoted to a senior director role and I have all of the confidence that Mike has "what it takes" to continue a great delivery tradition.

1. Complete 1994 product plans fast
2. Hire as planned (now that you have the approval) and attack performance problems
3. Demonstrate the "charisma" to lead—he's certainly demonstrated leadership ability
4. Get "the machine" in gear as planned by mid-year (project Bad Breath, Toad, etc.)
5. Support of common technology endeavors

Career Planning

Mike's taking on the Senior Director of Applications position is a huge step in his career. Mike will need to learn and grow in this position over the next few years in order to truly earn the right to advance to the next step—in charge of all of development.

Once the document is complete and you have verified it with both your boss (yeah, that's right) and the personnel department, you are ready to present the results to each of your managers.

Employee Surveys

Sometimes, the personnel department "rises from the dead" and decides to have an employee opinion survey (sometimes known as the dreaded "culture survey"). This is usually the opportunity for employees to respond to tough issues anonymously.

Should you take it seriously? Yes. It is a great way for employees and managers to evaluate their management and the company.

Rules for the Unruly

Rule 36: Don't perform your own employee survey.

Assume you have some extra time and you decide to construct your own survey. Don't do it. Why would anyone ever think of creating their own survey?

Well, at least one of my managers developed his own department survey and, amazingly, the manager (and the company) always "scored high," even though product results of the group was not the best.

If you were working for that manager, you would probably rate your manager fairly high, too!

Rule 37: Prioritize employee survey action items.

Why are your developers so apathetic towards filling out the survey when they are normally so outspoken? As I've been told before, no action ever comes from these surveys. No matter how well you as a manager have been evaluated, a few areas can always stand some improvement.

Rule 38: You don't have to resolve every survey issue.

Just because you receive employee feedback that may be fairly negative, there may be some requests that you, as the leader, must deny. For instance, you might respond by saying "No, this concern I feel we cannot change." As long as you communicate the reasons that you cannot fix a potential problem, you should still be credible with development.

Reality Checks

Check 19: Set the right expectation from prioritized survey action items.

Our organization always enjoyed positive employee surveys. However, we found that a few issues remained consistent among most surveys:

1. In order to improve productivity, there should be fewer meetings.
2. There is not enough communication between development and customer support.
3. The roles between project managers and senior design engineers are not clear and often become confrontational.

I had each of my managers take turns presenting the results of the employee survey. This showed our employees that each manager had a vested interest in the results; it wasn't just a summary from a personnel representative. Although we could have taken several hours, we simplified the presentation to take approximately one hour of everyone's time.

Next, we presented what the managers had prioritized as the major issues to be solved and why these issues were selected. We asked for development feedback and, not surprisingly, there were few comments.

Finally, we asked for representatives from development to work with each of my managers on each prioritized concern in order to jointly take action.

Whoa, this was interesting.

We made sure that each of my managers took a key concern and organized a task force to resolve each problem by turning the negative into a positive. All of these steps (from presentation to team sign-up) required only a single meeting!

Within three months, all the concerns had been resolved, with the results communicated back by the team to all of development.

I can't emphasize enough how critical this was:

1. Most of my peers didn't even bother with a formal presentation of the survey results to their groups.
2. Those who did review concerns with their troops let the personnel department perform the presentation. There can be no buy-in if you let a third party present the results!
3. Although, in a few cases, other organizations made promises to have management address employee concerns, little or no action really took place.

What does all of this say about the survey process? The next time the company performs a survey, few employees will want to take the time to fill it out. They saw no results before, so why bother again?

I think employee surveys are important. Well-designed surveys can illuminate the health of your organization—as long as the questionnaire asks meaningful questions that directly relate to your business. If the questions are so ambiguous that it is hard for employees to figure out how to answer, the survey is useless.

Practical Maniac Tips

Tip 15: Get the team to resolve critical survey items.

After the survey results have been summarized, follow up with your employees in this manner:

1. Gather your managers together with the personnel department and review the survey results. Everyone should force some level of prioritizing of major issues among themselves.
2. Review the results with all of your organization. Emphasize the critical issues that you and your managers have prioritized. The fewer you choose to respond to, the more impact the issues that you do choose will have!

In Summary

Reward stellar performance.

Even in development! Just do it right so that the individual, the company, and the team benefit from the results. Don't fall victim to incentives.

Advertise as if you were trying to hire yourself.

There is an art to making your classified advertisements attractive and effective. Disqualify "losers" or "posers" (in other words, development superstar wanna-be's) in the ad. Sometimes it helps to be a little humorous and direct in the ad. If you are too cocky, you might attract the dreaded "prima donna."

Set proper expectations during an interview.

No job or company is perfect. Describing your company to an applicant in nothing but glowing terms can lead to false expectations. I find it always good form to present both positive and negative aspects of the job and company. If you find that there are too many negatives, you may wish to find *yourself* another job.

Learn to deal with recruiters.

You just can't avoid them. Even if your company has a policy against using recruiters, you've got to figure out a way to get those killer prospects that they may represent. Recruiter fees are completely negotiable—they, too, need to make a living.

Even if you don't want to deal with recruiters, adopt a policy for handling them when they do call. And, believe me, a classified ad that says "Please, no recruiters" means nothing!

Career planning is crucial to keeping your best people long-term.

You don't have to learn how to do career planning from a textbook or seminars. Combining common sense and performance evaluations provides all the ingredients you need to help your best people feel like they have a future in your company.

Employee surveys are good medicine!

Think you've figured out your developers? Wait until your company unleashes the dreaded employee survey! Wow, the negative issues that arise can be tough to take. Your job, as a development leader, is to turn these negative concerns into positive change.

Becoming a Development Leader

*How do you know if you are truly the inspira-
tional leader that development needs? There is a
dramatic difference between managing and leading. For instance, technical proficiency isn't even
a key leadership trait. In fact, leading software
developers is really an art form, and one that you
should master. So, let me help demystify the art
of leading developers!*

This chapter will help you uncover those leadership traits that most of us possess (but often don't realize). In particular, I'll cover these topics:

- Recognizing leadership traits
- Leadership styles
- Working with marketing and sales executives
- Verifying that your leadership is working
- Absorbing another organization into development
- Rising through the ranks

Recognizing Leadership Traits

There are stacks of leadership books in print and I'm sure you've read some of the better ones. Yet these books don't seem to apply to the art of leading developers. They just don't seem to deal with the realities of this business. How did you become in charge?

A. Your boss died

B. A vote was taken and you won (or lost, depending on your perspective)

C. You were promoted through the ranks

D. You hired in as the manager

All but option C can have negative consequences, because you still have to prove your credibility with the developers that you will manage. If you were promoted through the ranks, you've probably already proved yourself to some extent, since management appears to have confidence in your abilities. In any case, you'll still have to display strong leadership abilities.

Do you recognize the leadership traits that will make you successful? Take a look at some of the traits that are commonly associated with leadership.

- **Desire for visibility.** You have a strong desire for acceptance and, after reading all of the trade magazines and noting the attention Bill Gates receives, you hunger for the same.

- **Ability to make correct decisions.** You've monitored the decisions made by previous management, and you're confident you can do a much better job.
- **You're well liked**. You're confident that, since you are well liked among development, teammanship can be emphasized.
- **You have a strong technology background.** Your strong technical skills will help rebuild credibility that was lacking in your predecessor.

If the above traits represent your reasons for advancing into development management, you will most likely fail. Consider each of these traits again (but this time, let me add some constructive advice):

Desire for Visibility

You won't have a problem being visible as a development manager. In fact, at times you'll wish you could "hide out." If you long for visibility, you would be better advised to run naked across the playing field during halftime at a Dallas Cowboys game.

Ability to Make Correct Decisions

Although you may feel certain that your predecessor failed at making well-informed decisions, you'll eventually find that, even when you have all the facts, making the so-called "correct decision" is still very difficult.

You're Well Liked

Of course, being "well hated" is not a requirement or even a desirable trait for any job. But if you believe the fact that you are well liked will help you win the confidence of developers, you are sadly mistaken. Great leadership is the only thing that will win the confidence of your developers. If you display great leadership, this implies that you are respected and sometimes well liked. In other words, a manager that is not necessarily liked is rarely an effective leader.

You Have a Strong Technology Background

This is not a leadership trait—*it is expected.*

If you can be "technically taken advantage of" by your developers, you are in serious trouble. You *must* know your field!

Okay. I've debunked some of the leadership myths that are common in high-tech industries. So, now you want to know what I *haven't* discussed: What *are* the great leadership traits?

Rules for the Unruly

Rule 39:   Recognize those leadership traits that are important.

In software development, I believe you must possess these leadership traits (in this order):

1. **Make well-informed decisions.** Making a decision too quickly or without the proper buy-in will pose a major credibility problem for you if your decision proves to be incorrect.

   Is there really ever a correct decision? I maintain that there is. In fact, there *always* is. Based on the circumstances at the time and the goals that surround the issue to be resolved, there is always a best decision.

   Decisions that affect the customer and the business can ruffle feathers if your developers do not agree with you. But if you have a reputation as a leader who makes sound decisions, this reputation will benefit both you and your organization.

2. **Cultivate the ability to listen.** If you find yourself controlling most of the conversation with your managers or teams, you are probably talking too much. How can you tell?

   - Frequent "dry mouth"
   - Headaches
   - Folks you talk with look uninterested
   - You frequently forget the topic you initially were discussing

   If you've already advanced successfully in your chosen field, you don't need to constantly prove your knowledge. Relax. This is your opportunity to let others be the experts. Your job is to get the most out of your folks. Let them tell you what *they* know!

3. **Communicate (that is, stay "in touch" with development).**
Being in touch with development means that you are aware of the major risk factors affecting delivery of projects and that everyone's role is clear.

If you can't answer the basic question "What could negatively affect the delivery of each of your projects?" then you're in trouble! In addition, if you have difficulty communicating and would rather not spend your time communicating with your folks, you may want to reevaluate your career options. I've seen some pretty good development managers who didn't enjoy "walkin' the talk" with the development troops. As a result, the developers could only guess what was on the manager's mind. They frequently guessed wrong.

If your development team members aren't entirely sure what their roles and accountabilities are, there is little chance that your folks will take care of situations that "fall through the cracks". In developing projects, there are too many chances for things to go wrong! And they usually do go wrong before they go right.

Are there more traits? Of course, but these three are simple to remember and are the most important.

Rule 40: There is a difference between managing and leading.

Rather than compare the differences between managers and leaders, I would like to characterize us all as managers responsible for our business endeavors and personnel.

Our ability to control and administrate development activities is understood. That's the basis of our job. To avoid any misunderstanding, I'll list the job functions that will appear on almost all job descriptions:

- Stay within budget
- Handle performance reviews
- Hire and terminate
- Attend and manage meetings
- Keep track of project status and employee performance

At a minimum, we are expected to maintain our business. I have found that most beginning development managers can do this pretty well. The preceding list describes functions that are required *only* to maintain the business. By incorporating these functions into your job, your business should continue in an evolutionary fashion. By "business," I refer to both development as well as your company as a whole.

In other words, development *is* a business. And development is one of the only areas of a company that can truly revolutionize the company. Sales can't. Marketing can't. Finance can't. And let's face it, development's business is to deliver products on schedule. You have schedules to meet, hiring to do, performance to evaluate, customers to satisfy, and budgets to keep. As a result, too often development managers treat development as nothing more than an expense cost center while the rest of the company may view development as a liability without much fiscal control.

So how do you escape that trap and instead *revolutionize* your business? The activities below are potential ways to dramatically energize your business:

- Use key third-party technologies in order to reengineer products for faster delivery.
- Adopt automation techniques that can help your customers repeat common activities (i.e., batch processing).
- With neural networks and fuzzy logic coming on strong, maybe you can keep customers excited about your product lines by adopting some of these knowledge-based technologies.
- With some forethought, you can make products primarily geared for the United States market suitable for use outside the U.S. (where most of the high growth potential is).

I could add to the list, but that's really your job. It's amazing how ideas can develop once you push yourself to think "outside of the box." This is a great sign of development leadership over and above management. (By the way, more information on technology appears in Chapter 9.)

Rule 41: Development leadership shouldn't fall into the "teaching trap."

I have seen overzealous development managers attempt informal "teaching sessions" where once a week, for example, staff members present something technically exciting to development. This can be extremely motivating as long as you have decent attendance. On the other hand, you are dealing with developers, who tend to be antisocial and cynical of anything that is "organized." So, how can you get decent attendance?

I've seen one of my managers make these weekly meetings mandatory. And, of course, it doesn't take but a few weeks before people are looking for excuses to miss the meetings. This is definitely discouraging to managers who think that these sessions were "asked for by the developers themselves."

The amount of preparation it takes for developers to put together demonstrations can be enormous. Here are some guidelines to follow if you decide to offer so-called "learning sessions":

- Do not make learning sessions a regular event—as soon as they become regular, they lose their punch.

- If you really need to present something interesting, add the presentation to your regularly scheduled development meeting rather than set up yet another learning meeting. That way, everyone can enjoy the presentation.

- Make the learning sessions extremely short—no more than 20 to 30 minutes.

- Look for a notable speaker or "visionary" from neighboring companies who could be a guest inspiration. I have found that guest speakers from Borland or Microsoft can motivate development about interesting topics in the software industry.

- Communicate ad hoc newsworthy items that might otherwise go completely unnoticed. When I travel and realize that the new copy of *PC Week* has been delivered to my office, I go crazy. So my secretary express mails the magazine to me while I'm on the road. I can't tell you how many times I've read something interesting while on the road, later passed the information on to the development staff, and a seemingly trivial article becomes the basis for a product or new technology.

I've found critical information about application frameworks, desktop publishing tools, debuggers, and network security products through magazines. I insist on an environment where interesting articles are copied and passed around in order to invigorate some thinking outside of our current tool or technology methods.

This does not have to be a boring business!

I have found interesting magazine commentaries that have helped me prove important points with my peers in marketing. Examples have been:

- Importance of great documentation as it relates to effective customer support
- The role of user interface testing with new products
- The coming age of platform-independent software development
- Creating products from software building blocks

Reality Checks

Check 20: Recognize yourself as a leader.

One of my managers was frustrated with the company and my leadership. At a dinner meeting, he stated very boldly:

"You know, Ken, no one really knows what you or development stands for. You demonstrate no leadership."

I didn't even know how to respond. How dare he?

One of my other managers was at the table and she suggested, after the manager left the table, that we "ought to fire his ass." His comment really hurt. However, if I was in a developer's shoes and I didn't see "leadership" being practiced, I would probably agree with the frustrated manager.

Obviously, being a development leader requires that you have a "thick skin" and the ability to take constructive criticism. From that day on, I always pretended that development needed to constantly be reassured of a manager's leadership. Even if you earn the mantle of "leader," you're not set for life. I find that it *constantly* needs to be earned.

As an example, I make sure that I:

- Continue to make well-informed decisions and get proper buy-in with my management team
- Communicate good *and* bad news
- Stay in touch with the top two or three risks of *every* project
- Consistently make decisions based on customer (i.e., the market) needs first and company business next

Check 21: I should have asked my managers first.

Ever been thrown into a problem that you've had no experience dealing with? There is nothing like that feeling! How about this example:

My boss decided to close a very important development contract that had lingered throughout the executive and legal organization forever. Well, it seemed like forever.

The deal would be one of the most momentous technology partnerships the company had ever known. Press statements were issued, and there were speeches, contract parties, and hoopla! Yee hah! Our competition was definitely taken by surprise. Times like these make being in the software development business worthwhile.

But there was a problem.

I was never consulted before the deal. By the time marketing saw the contract, it was determined that there was no apparent way we were ever going to make any money—no matter how many copies of the product we sold!

The project was eventually terminated after millions of dollars were spent. The company could have saved a lot of negative exposure if senior management had been collectively consulted prior to the partnership.

Practical Maniac Tips

Tip 16: Create a list of management and leadership actions with your managers.

Table 3.1 shows a few sample items that you and your managers can use as examples.

Table 3.1 Sample management versus leadership worksheet

Issue	Management action	Leadership action
Budgets	Stay within budget	Reevaluate people's skills and retrain to bring project in 10 percent under budget
Performance reviews	Make sure that all reviews are done on time	Perform joint mini-reviews once a month

continued

Table 3.1 Sample management versus leadership worksheet (continued)

Issue	Management action	Leadership action
Attrition	Keep performance reviews on track to avoid needless attrition	Do whatever it takes to bring attrition to within 10% of our current headcount

You can almost consider the management actions to be synonymous with normal maintenance activities, while leadership actions could be synonymous with high growth, high risk activities.

The goal is to train everyone (including yourself) to solve issues with leadership ferocity wherever possible. It's not unusual to make decisions that have a fair amount of risk attached!

Adopting a Leadership "Style"

Is there such a thing as "developing a style"? Well, I frequently tell people that two things contribute to my style :

1. I watch Oliver Stone's *Platoon* and Francis Coppola's *Godfather* videos in order to "fine tune" my leadership skills.
2. I reread Tracy Kidder's *Soul of a New Machine* every year to understand how to "handle developers."

In actual fact, I doubt if anyone working with me would characterize my management style as anything resembling the above sources. But I enjoy the videos because they really represent how difficult decision making is in a team or stressful environment. Kidder's book provides an excellent lesson in how *not* to treat developers.

Actions speak louder than words, and although you can't really proclaim what your style is, it will not take long before people perceive what your style actually is *for you*:

"He's never really predictable or consistent."
"I wish she would listen to us."
"I never quite know where I stand."

Rules for the Unruly

Rule 42: Participate and be recognized as part of the team.

Since development is only as strong as your teammanship and leadership skills, you need to be a key part of the team. In other words:

- If you don't know how to operate your products, you had better learn. The worse thing that can happen to a development leader is to be viewed as an administrator and not as a knowledgeable leader.

- Periodically, step into your team meetings and, most of all, listen. At key points, make sure that your presence and appreciation of the team's problems are made clear. You'll be able to tell that you have the respect of the team if they ask you questions. If after several meetings, you are just "part of the scenery," your own role may not be well understood or appreciated.

Rule 43: Lead by example.

When you need your folks to work long hours (see Reality Check 23 later in this chapter), take the pain, too. It doesn't help if your folks work all weekend and you don't even participate. You can actually make things worse if you make a "guest appearance" for only 30 minutes while your folks struggle all weekend.

Rule 44: Delegate effectively.

Most development managers have great difficulty giving up the reins to allow their managers to properly run their organizations. If you don't have strong managers working for you, then how will you succeed?

Your leadership is dependent on you, but your effectiveness depends on the strength of your managers and teams. The phrase "You are only as good as your people" holds true. Even if this means removing someone from a key role.

Rule 45: Use your time well.

If your goal is to be in meetings only some of the time, then be available when you are not in those meetings. If your goal is to be available to your teams, then verify that you really are available. Chances are that you're not as available as you think. See the Reality Check 26 later in this chapter.

Reality Checks

Check 22: Roll out the red carpet, there's a new guy in town.

If you are hired into a new role, chances are you will be treated not with "hail to the King" (in other words, Elvis) but more like "what are you doing here?" One development leader came in with:

- Tons of ideas and lots of energy
- Management disciplines he wanted to start immediately
- A technical strategy
- A "bashing philosophy" of previous management

Nothing wrong with that, right? But it was odd that he hadn't bothered to talk with any of the staff before adopting the above mentality. The result? There was absolutely no credibility in anything that he expounded. It took him several months to finally learn to listen and to use his staff effectively since he almost "burned all bridges" initially.

If you are new to a position and the previous management's success was in the least bit questionable, tread carefully. Talk is cheap—results are not.

Check 23: Deal directly with obstinate employees no matter who they are.

How do you handle employees who do not wish to contribute or are constantly a pain to manage? Ignoring the problem employee will not help matters. You must find out if the employee has truly "signed up."

The next paragraph is very important.

I find myself constantly placing developers into the "real world." Rather than lecture the individual, I want the employee to "own the problem" as if it were his or her own company. For example, to get Mary to agree to work through the weekend, I could take a couple of approaches:

"We need you to work through the weekend. Everyone else pulls their own weight, why can't you? The company needs you."

or . . .

"I know you may not have much faith that the company cares if you work the weekend. But, I guarantee if it was your company and your company's future needed some extra effort, you'd make it happen. The team really needs your help—the company is depending on you. You *are* the company!"

It is often very easy for employees to forget that they are more a part of the company than just an employee getting a paycheck. By the way, I know that more companies these days are calling employees "associates" or "contributors." These fancy names do not mean a lot if management doesn't create an atmosphere where everyone is empowered and responsible for the company's success.

Teamwork and communication, encouraged from a leader (meaning you), can really help. Stock incentives and ownership options can seal an employee's sense of ownership in the company.

Check 24: Showing anger does not work.

We've all seen situations where managers exert so-called "management by intimidation." Anger or the use of four-letter words may add some color to a meeting, but someone in the room will usually be offended.

I've seen a case where a senior engineer got so upset with a decision that he grabbed a phone and threw it into a wall while chanting four-letter words, apparently hoping that someone in the room would be intimidated enough to modify the decision.

Techniques like this appear to show immaturity and noncredibility because developers typically make decisions in a very logical way. Anger and intimidation doesn't help developers work harder or even smarter.

Although I can't speak for developers everywhere, in my view anger never achieves results. It doesn't work with children, teenagers, or software professionals.

Point of fact: The one time in my life when I got angry while driving occurred when someone didn't signal and cut me off. I then smacked the horn.

I thought it was the horn.

I was driving a rental car and had smacked my windshield wipers instead. I couldn't believe it. I had to pull over until I could stop laughing.

Check 25: Remove people who are not effective.

Are you ready for a big lesson?

One of my senior managers was the inventor of key technologies that had brought the company much fame and success. It was this type of individual that the company really needed. Without his innovation, there would probably not have been a company when I joined.

Anyway, he had been promoted to a senior management position in development and was responsible for leading his teams to the "next plateau" of products. He had plenty of ideas and was still considered a visionary.

The problem was that his teams were not getting anything done. Every time he had an idea, he would brainstorm it with his team. And, of course, each of these ideas was very important and would dramatically improve customer satisfaction.

Because of his stature, I felt that it would be a real problem to take him off his current responsibility. He had earned it and, if he was "demoted," he might quit. My boss was not happy with the team's progress, but I didn't have the heart (or guts) to remove him.

My boss intervened and moved the development manager off the project and into a "visionary" (i.e., staff thinker) role. The team was actually happy and wished that it had taken place months before. The manager was not thrilled but eventually was actually relieved.

He hadn't been enjoying his role because of the stress!

The moral of the story: Do the right thing for the project and for the company even if it is a difficult personal decision. Your success depends on your folks being effective at the right job. If your folks are not successful, *you* will not be successful.

Check 26: Spend your time efficiently.

I could spend several chapters on time management. In fact, time management is such a fundamental issue that I want to make sure the importance of time management is always in your mind. The pie chart in Figure 3.1 shows what I think my use of time *should be*.

I wanted a majority of my time to be used for planning and for unplanned activities. So, I kept track of my time for one month. This was easy. The pie chart in Figure 3.2 shows what my time actually was.

The percentages were strangely the same, but the *use* of time was dramatically different. I had little time available to handle unplanned activities. The majority of my time was taken up with travel and meetings. Just the opposite of what I had hoped for! What does this say about my time management?

The point is that I might not have realized how off the mark my time management was if I hadn't taken the time to track my use of time. The best thing you can do is learn from your misuse of time and do something about it.

Figure 3.1 Desired time use

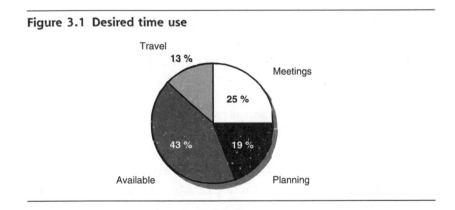

Figure 3.2 Actual use of time

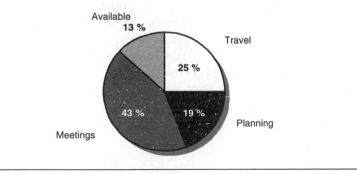

Practical Maniac Tips

Tip 17: Test to see if you spend time wisely.

Just so you really know how you spend your time, keep a list of your time over the next few weeks. Although you can use categories that fit your business needs, the following categories should represent a majority of your actual time used:

- Meetings
- Planning
- Available for anything

Before keeping track of your time, write the percentages that you want to have for each time category. Your calendar is the perfect notebook to use to track how your time is spent. Once you've compiled the totals and computed percentages, look at what you currently use versus what you originally wanted.

If the percentages (desired and actual) are the same, you should be teaching a course in time management. If they are significantly different, make changes in your schedule to adjust your use of time closer to your targets.

Tip 18: Make sure your managers use their time well.

After you've made sure your own time management is in decent shape, perform the same exercise with your management team. There is nothing so revealing as comparing time management perception to actual practice in a team setting.

Tip 19: Your managers must know their products.

To make sure that you and your managers know your product lines, have your managers demonstrate to you the operation of the products they are responsible for. Ask plenty of questions.

Learn the basics of each product and make sure that you can demonstrate each of your products (at least in a basic mode of operation). Who knows? You may be asked questions about your products from your customers one day. It happens.

Working with Other Executives

Ever feel uncomfortable being in development when your friends or peers are in other, more notable businesslike positions?

You should.

Development is typically regarded by mainstream business managers as an organization "out of control." I've found that the following basic rules, if handled correctly, can help build camaraderie among you and managers within other business functions. And they don't require you to learn to play golf!

Rules for the Unruly

Rule 46: Treat development as a business unit.

If you constantly defend development as something special or as a sanctuary for cultural misfits, your approach may be humorous to other managers.

At first.

If and when development has difficulty delivering products to market on schedule, the humor evaporates rather quickly. Don't be afraid to present objective views of your own staff and, if there are problems, admit them. Then present action items that inspire confidence within your peers that you have the ability to solve these problems.

I can't tell you how often I've heard presidents and CEOs say something similar to:

"I wish we could figure out how to get the development people under control. My own VP of development can't seem to figure them out."

Rule 47: Keep yourself oriented toward "customer first."

The number one priority for most companies is to satisfy customer needs. So, if you make yourself available for customer presentations, it can help reinforce the fact that development also considers customers to be the highest priority.

What can you talk about with other, non-development managers? How about these for starters:

• Technical strategy

- Reviews of the industry
- A synopsis of the procedures you follow to take product ideas from "cradle to grave"

Rule 48: Keep "touchy/feely" sessions to a minimum.

An overzealous strategy consultant or personnel organization may wish to impose what I call "touchy/feely" management team building. Unless you are experienced in psychology, stepping in on sessions like these can destroy teammanship or trust rather than help it.

Rule 49: Present "Their Side" to development.

Sometimes, difficult decisions that have been solved with your management peers will have to be presented to development. Presenting unpopular decisions can be very difficult if you know that developers will take the decision in a negative fashion.

You've no doubt heard of situations where an executive has been nuked (I mean, terminated) and the development folks stage a protest out in the parking lot.

Get real!

The last thing you should do is to blame "them" (management) for the decision. Simply explain the situation to your folks, explain why it is a difficult decision, and then get people's understanding (in order to reduce "after meeting rumoring"). Try to get development to view the decision as one that is best for the company as a whole. You may never gain people's agreement of the action but you should be able to gain their understanding.

Reality Checks

Check 27: Stay away from those "touchy/feely" performance sessions.

When a team of managers (or executives) is not acting as a team and results are not taking place as everyone expects, what do you do?

An interesting situation happened to me when, through the use of management consultants, our management team met at an off-site location in order to get in touch with each other's performance.

Harmless so far, right?

When we started our meeting, all of the executives sat in a circle. For each executive present, the others were to explain what he or she did well or poorly. Each executive under scrutiny would then have to respond in a positive way. This openness was supposed to remove "barriers" and to solve deep-seated problems. I couldn't believe what I was hearing (I thought back to "peace and love" clichés from the 60s), but I had no choice except to participate.

Here's an example of Richard's turn at bat:

"Richard, we delivered the product to your sales force and my folks were disappointed because your crew didn't even know the product. You offer little leadership and I know by way of rumors that you are not trusted. In fact, I don't really trust you anymore."

"Tom, <gulp> thanks for your feedback. I admit that I could have trained my folks better but we just received the product two weeks ago. I will work with my managers to put together a plan to address the training issue. With regard to the leadership issue you brought up, give me a chance to prove that sales numbers will dramatically improve next month."

What Richard really wants to say is:

"Tom, you jerk. We didn't even know when you were going to actually ship the product since we saw you fail three times in a row. You have no idea how hard it is to work with sales folks. I'm gonna see that you roast in Hell for this humiliation."

I've witnessed sessions like this and played a part in several. I've seen executives lose their jobs at sessions like this. You may think this example sounds unreal and couldn't happen, but believe me, it does!

 ## Practical Maniac Tips

Tip 20: Pay close attention to how you present difficult news.

Try this approach the next time a difficult decision has to be made. Before you have to explain the situation to your development troops, discuss the circumstances with your managers and make sure that you all have planned for any potential negative feed-back—before the communication.

After the communication, review how well it went with your managers. Remind your managers that, any time they have to be involved with potentially volatile communication, you and your management team are prepared for the worst.

Handling difficult communication is part of our job and is a skill that is not easy to master. Anyone can mishandle difficult communication—correcting poor communication after the fact requires a longer time period and really hurts your credibility with development.

Verifying your Leadership Effectiveness

How do you determine whether you are really an effective leader? That's a tricky question. Consider the following qualities that you *should* have. Specifically, development needs a leader who:

- Acts and is perceived as the development spokesperson
- Can break log jams and offer creative ways to solve problems
- Is in touch with the issues that development faces and who is not afraid to defend development (when it makes sense) but will "temper" development's naive views (when development is clearly wrong)

Rules for the Unruly

Rule 50: Make every effort to remind your folks that you are the leader.

Development needs someone who demonstrates the following traits (compared to the development folks): more crazy, more mature, more a listener, more a talker, more technical, more technically dependent on the staff, more serious, and funny (at the right time). I know this list is rife with contradictions, but leadership doesn't fit neatly in a box. You know how developers think—emulate them and, at the same time, rise above them.

Your folks need that personality mixture in a leader. Picture a CFO as VP of development—it just won't happen; no personality. Picture your CEO as VP of development—too much stress. Picture your VP of marketing as VP of development—no credibility.

Picture yourself as the VP of development: what would developers think? (If you are already VP of development, what do you think your developers *really* think?)

Rule 51: Solve difficult problems by taking personal excursions.

Some of the best thoughts can come to you away from work. For example, when I had problems with our documentation not meeting the needs of customer support, I couldn't figure out how to solve the problem. I was watching kids play at a playground and I noticed two kids arguing until a third kid came over and calmed them down. From that moment on, the three played great together.

I immediately came to the conclusion that I needed one boss in charge of both departments with the single goal of setting them to work together to improve this huge problem. This "excursion" of taking a totally unrelated incident and using it to relate to solving a work-related problem, happens to me all of the time. I'm not the only one (although most people don't admit to this method of problem solving).

Rule 52: Take "Excursions" to solve difficult problems.

I am constantly finding that difficult problems can be solved by making connections with subjects that have little to do with the product. This association is a key element to creative software design. For example, modern software uses innovative graphics to emulate everyday activity. Before, software was restricted to a textual form of interface.

In case you've forgotten, software is not an entity in itself—its sole purpose is to automate cumbersome real-world activities. This fact applies to accounting systems that have taken the place of error-prone ledger books as well as to art departments that now put together presentations on a laptop computer five minutes before a speech.

Use excursions to improve not only product design but to solve management problems. You may fail at "excursions" (especially if you are not a trained facilitator) but the exercise is well worth it.

 **Reality Checks**

Check 28: Demonstrate leadership outside of the norm.

I really believe in "going the extra mile" in order to prove that you, as a development leader, are not only a part of the development frenzy but can lead no matter what the odds.

I find that developers tend to like strange stories. Here's one.

I was to meet my managers at the airport for a flight to a very important customer meeting the next morning. This was the last flight that day to the customer's destination. I had all of the presentation material and was the only one who knew how to get to the customer's site. I left the office 40 minutes before the flight in order to complete some last-minute office work.

Some folks arrive at the airport a couple of hours before their flight in order to catch up on "bar talk." Not me—I always try to get in some additional work before the flight. In fact, I had developed a reputation for just barely making flight departures, so most folks did not enjoy traveling with me.

Since it took approximately 20 minutes to drive to the airport, I figured I had plenty of time. Well, I was driving down the road and my steering wheel froze. I pulled over and I remembered . . .

I forgot to put fuel in my car that morning. My car had run out of gas!

Oh, man. I couldn't believe it! Five minutes had already passed. I spent about 15 seconds reciting words that I would never use in public and pounded the steering column.

I got out of the car, turned to face the traffic and did what any normal American would do: stuck up my thumb. After about two minutes, I was picked up by two women and a dog in a pickup truck. Since they had no room in the cabin, I sat outside in the back holding on to the sides.

There I was—clad in suit and tie, and holding on for dear life as the woman behind the wheel drove like a maniac to get me to the service station. I thanked them as they dropped me off. They sped off as I jumped out.

Fortunately, the service station wasn't busy with other customers. I ran inside and told the attendant what had happened. He said he would be glad to help as long as I put a $5 deposit on the gas can. I paid him and ran out to pump the gas. I then asked if I could get a ride to my car, which was only about one mile down the road.

Next to the attendant was a helper who had been observing the situation. The attendant said, "I can't afford to use Jerry over thar, you'll have to find your own way."

I said, "Yeah, but, he's not busy!"

The response I got was straight from The Andy Griffith Show: "If Jerry helped ya and a customer came in to get gas, who would pump the gas?"

Well, I couldn't argue with that logic.

So, I ran out to the road with a five-gallon container of gas in one hand and my thumb hiked up on the other. I got a ride again, and this guy brought me right to my car. Already 20 minutes had passed.

I poured the gas into the car, stomped on the accelerator, and "flew" back to the service station to return the gas container.

I was sure going to get my $5 deposit back!

Then off I went to park my car and absolutely run to a plane that was about 30 seconds from closing the doors.

Whew! The story is true and most people would have just given up and missed the flight. I couldn't because of my responsibilities to my managers and to this meeting—I *had* to make that flight.

Check 29: Think "out of the box."

I am constantly finding that difficult problems have solutions that are usually unrelated to the problem. For example, if you are constructing a product strategy, it is easy to start forcing your strategy on your current products and customer needs.

The problem with this approach: You are starting with a knowledge base that is based on what you already know.

I can only imagine that, when Shapeware came up with the idea for ViSiO, their original intent was to create a software product that was aimed at providing basic drawing tools for the masses. Knowing that plenty of software drawing tools are available now, what approach would be more effective (since software drawing tools tend to be far too complicated in operation for most people to use)?

A good strategic consultant could take the management team and have them look at other, completely unrelated topics. Here are some examples:

"What did you enjoy most at school?"

"Looking outside the window, what key objects interest you?"

Consider the first question about school. One of the management team could have answered, "Mathematics, I really enjoyed working with protractors and slide rules." Another could have said, "Art, using brushes and watercolors was my favorite."

See any resemblance yet?

Now let me follow up with yet another question. "Is there any way to associate the use of tools you all used in mathematics and art that could help customers use a software drawing tool?"

"Well, " says one of the managers, "instead of drawing common symbols by hand, if we provided a stencil much like the stencil I used in school, it would be much easier for customers to select the symbol over and over."

Another manager followed, "Yeah, the old flowchart template would be a perfect metaphor to display next to a drawing tablet."

And thus, a star is born. This sequence may not have been even remotely close to how Shapeware thought of their stencil metaphor, but you can see how ideas are associated from the most unlikely subject. Can you imagine how your "favorite class in school" could have helped construct the excellent "stencil template" implementation used in ViSiO?

Practical Maniac Tips

Tip 21: **Practice ways to solve problems outside of the norm.**

Select one of your projects that is losing market share within a still-expanding market.

Just because you are losing market share does not mean you can't compete!

Take your development management team (along with marketing) to an off-site location. Run through several excursions in order to truly brainstorm some creative ways to re-energize the product (and the team).

By the way, if people are not "loose enough" to be creative, I find that beer is a superb stimulus.

In Summary

Make sure you demonstrate leadership traits that will make you successful.

These include:

- An ability to listen
- Making well-informed decisions
- Communicating and staying in touch with development

Make sure that you delegate.

If you have an organization that cannot be successful without your everyday presence, chances are that the managers who report to you aren't ones you can count on. Delegation is a strength, not a weakness!

Manage your time.

Make sure that your development goals are matched by the way you control your time.

Treat development like a business unit.

You must make sure that development is not viewed as "outside of the normal business," with no customer orientation. If you really do think that development should be treated separately and should naturally be highly regarded, look for a job at a university. In the business world, you'll never last with that attitude.

The Development Team

Who belongs on the development team? It's commonplace for engineering to be considered the same as development. In reality, this just isn't true!

If you thought you were successful, yet you feel strangely "out of touch" with the development folks, read this chapter. The contents may surprise you, especially if you haven't realized that the signals you project as a leader of developers can produce either successful or disastrous results. I'll discuss the following topics:

- Defining development teams
- Changing the size of teams, management hierarchies, and the infamous "team minutes"
- Behaving with your peers (and how to be more credible)
- Managing interesting team dynamics

Who Makes Up a Development Team?

Consider the relationships among the disciplines within the software development organization. Specifically, take a look at the relationships among the groups shown in Figure 4.1.

Although I'm sure you know what each of these organizations does, let's review them briefly to make sure you understand how I'm using the terms.

- **Software engineering:** The organization that is responsible for designing and implementing software projects.
- **Quality assurance:** The organization (SQA, for short) that is responsible for testing software projects.

Figure 4.1 The development organization

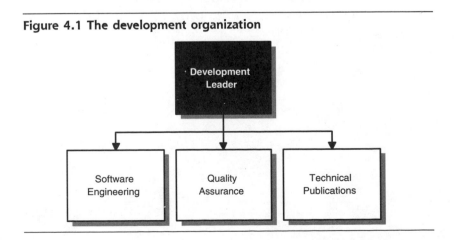

- **Technical publications:** The organization (i.e., documentation) that is responsible for the creation of document related material and on-line assistance.

Your role as the development leader requires you to quickly come to terms with the way these organizations interact. For instance, when key decisions have to be made, how do you treat conflicting information you may hear from each of these three organizations?

Managing the relationships among these groups may be your biggest challenge. To understand why I say this, take a tour of each organization.

Software Engineering

Engineering is the group whose main responsibility is the specifications and implementation of a project. These are the folks who program in software languages and frequently are overheard talking about such esoteric terms as bit, objects, baud rates, and member functions. When they look busy, they are frequently typing in frenzy mode. When they look like they are not busy, they are probably doing their best thinking and planning.

An individual from another organization may assume that engineers are not working however, it is usually because the engineers' fingers aren't typing!

Software engineers tend to work better alone. However, when they finally understand how to take advantage of team cooperation, the best programmers' performance should get even better.

Quality should be owned by engineering. Even though there should be a specific quality organization, engineering should take pride in providing error-free product for final testing. Too often, engineers take the attitude that SQA just means "pass software over the wall" to the eagerly waiting testers.

If the number of bugs encountered during a development project number in the hundreds or even thousands, chances are you have sloppy programmers. The amount of time it takes to isolate problems is huge, and the more that are caught by the original engineer, the better the project results will be!

In my experience, some of the best engineers are those with either a musical or, you won't believe this, an electrical engineering background! Creative, yet analytical.

Software Quality Assurance

The SQA testing organization is the group that owns quality results—they are the spokespeople for "might and right." A product doesn't ship, as far as I'm concerned, unless SQA says it is ready!

Marketing generally doesn't appreciate the role of SQA testers because they determine when a product ships. In addition it is a fatal mistake for development management to make it appear that SQA's time to test is the critical item that keeps a project from timely completion. Given the information that it will take eight weeks from beta to release, marketing will almost invariably ask for that to be cut in half.

In reality, testing's role is to safeguard the customer from subsequent fatal product recalls and erratic program behavior. Testing organizations that are composed of power users will generally not provide very good "code coverage"—in fact, the introduction of automated test technology (where computers use scripts to test other computers executing the product) has been a lifesaver for many companies. The rest of the development team (and marketing for that matter) should take special care in evaluating a tester's test plan for accuracy and product coverage. A poor test plan will waste everyone's time and certainly won't find critical problems.

You will never find 100 percent of a software project's problems—but you can prioritize your test plan to find the majority of problems lurking in engineers' code. I really marvel at those organizations where engineers help testers as follows:

1. Engineers execute their own tests with each module before their contribution is integrated with the rest of the project.
2. Engineers provide module test points (sometimes in the form of an API) that a tester can then use to write tests which controls and validates the operation of the module.

Testers are frequently under incredible stress, so handle them with kid gloves. Good testers are worth their weight in gold and, like documentation, there is more to a tester's job description than meets the eye. Here are some examples of specific testing positions over and above the normal procedures that test the products day in and day out:

- Test designers
- Test coordinators and supervisors
- Testers who help train sales personnel and customers in the proper use of the product

Testers should be regarded as highly critical team participants and treated with respect—*not* as second class citizens that engineering barely tolerates. It is your job as development leader to reinforce the value of strict testing and quality discipline.

I find that support personnel with a strong technical ability become the best testers. Frustrated engineers-turned-testers tend to be "problem children." If a software engineer is not performing to expectations, you may consider moving him (or her) to a testing role. This action, as logical as it sounds, usually fails because it looks like a "step down" to the engineer and a "slap in the face" to the other quality assurance folks.

Technical Publications

The documentation (alias technical publications) organization is the "eyes and ears" for development.

Documentors must perform magic: Transforming a continually changing piece of technology into an easy-to-understand piece of literature.

Oh, did I mention that the documentation must be completed before the product ships?

That's why it's crazy for documentation to be a part of any organization other than development. Documentation can dramatically aid in the product development process by performing the following services (over and above writing manuals):

- help design the user interface and test the product's usability
- perform rapid prototyping
- verify that product designs can be easily interpreted for customer use
- create specifications and interpretations of specifications
- perform product overviews and build demonstrations
- create training materials

I find that the documentation group offers a "breath of fresh air" because they are more user-focused than technology-focused. They tend to have one weakness, though: Sometimes documentors care more about the "look and feel" of the documentation aids and care less about the content.

And don't think that the only job description in this organization is "writer." There are all sorts of documentation positions (depending on the need):

• user interface designer

• editor

• publications manager (handling the logistics of printing and typesetting)

• on-line help and multimedia designer

• language translator

With the rising costs of customer support to software providers (such as yourself), great documentation will dramatically reduce phone support requirements. Poor documentation will guarantee huge phone support needs.

The most effectively designed documentation can really help your product become successful and, of course, satisfy your customers. I've definitely seen cases where, even though a software product has had some problems, the documentation presented a thorough and realistic expectation. Devoting an entire mini-book on troubleshooting techniques can really help the customer understand what should be in the basic documentation package:

• Great on-line information

• A quick reference guide

• A manual that explains everything

A customer can become very confused when presented with several different errata sheets each explaining why the documentation isn't exactly accurate.

And whatever you do, make sure that your documentation page design is easy on the eyes. Some software companies still don't understand that thin-stroked, 9-point fonts really hurt the eyes after about ten minutes of reading.

Rules for the Unruly

Rule 53: Make the teams equal in status.

From this point on, the organization I call development includes engineering, SQA, and documentation. It is critical that you communicate the fact that all organizations need to participate on equal status in the making of decisions—the "tie breaker" (or the one with the most influence to evaluate conflicts) is *you*, not engineering!

There may be considerable pay differences among the groups due to market demand. Pay differentials have no bearing on someone's value to the team. Don't be afraid to communicate that fact to development. Too often, the pay ranges tend to support the idea that engineering should have the ultimate "say so."

Rule 54: Enforce the status quo.

It is one thing to make speeches about the equal status among members of the various development disciplines. It is another matter to execute and stand by that commitment. If your product release decisions are based solely on engineering's viewpoint when SQA is vocally against that viewpoint, you have already sabotaged the status quo.

This does not suggest that you must gain 100-percent consensus with all groups involved when making a decision. I'm just saying that, in order to make a well-informed decision, you had better have all three organizations available to participate in the decision process.

Rule 55: Educate marketing on roles.

Even when you get your internal organization working well as a team, you will still have a fight on your hands if marketing doesn't understand it or even buy into your "equal status" philosophy.

So educate marketing. Explain why your teams work on equal status but also reinforce your commitment to provide one key participant as your team's leader and spokesperson: the engineering project manager.

Rule 56: Enforce a career path for all of development.

A key demotivator is for your employees to think that they have no future except to advance into management. As individual contributors, they need to feel like they can be promoted into—an architect role that has the same visibility and importance as managers (see Figure 4.2). Don't forget to work on a set of job descriptions that are similar in responsibility among all development disciplines.

Rule 57: Other organizations are equally important.

I would like to emphasize some other organizations that should be brought into the development process as critical participants:

Customer support The customer support group plays a very valuable role in the product development process. I have specifically lumped documentation and customer support under one manager because I am convinced that the better the documentation, the better will be customer satisfaction. Again, the end result is fewer customer support calls.

Distribution (i.e. Fulfillment) If you have never "shrink wrapped" materials used in the final building of products, I suggest that you get a quick education. It is tedious work, but if distribution is a part of the development organization (again, I like distribution to be a part of documentation), then last minute "oops I forgot" situations are less likely to occur.

Distribution should be given enough lead time before customer shipment to plan for the following:

- Gain approval of complete bill of materials
- Virus detection of master diskettes
- Special options required for any potential custom orders

Figure 4.2 Dual career path

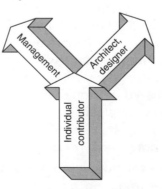

- Ensuring that customer databases can accommodate the new product. (If you get distribution involved at beta, you can attempt a "trial run.")

Legal assistance Why care about legal and archival details when you have a product to release? Well, there have been cases—very embarrassing situations—where a product is released without proper verification of potential naming conflicts with other products already in the market. There are also cases where there has not been proper validation of required royalty or legal notices when your product uses third-party software components.

And the biggest nightmare: Development neglects to archive the project in a way that will allow you to recreate it months if not years later. If you don't have someone specifically assigned to be responsible for these activities, issues will "fall through the cracks."

And *that* is a horrible lesson to learn! Read on.

 ## Reality Checks

Check 30: Sure, I can recreate the product!

A few years after we had released a major product into the market, we received a call from an irate customer who was totally dissatisfied with the newer versions of our software. They were actually willing to pay big bucks for some minor enhancements to an earlier version.

Big bucks.

Great. We located a couple of outside consultants who could perform the software development so that none of my in-house developers would have to leave their current assignments. This was definitely a win/win (win for us, win for the customer) situation!

I sent our newly created archival person—I like the title development coordinator—to search our vaults for the source code. *She couldn't find it!*

What?

Fortunately, the engineering project manager had a copy of the source code in his desk drawer. But it was only luck that prevented a disaster. From that point on, we made sure that a project was not finished until it was properly archived.

Practical Maniac Tips

Tip 22: Agree on rules and responsibilities.

Provide a forum where you and your managers can agree on a status quo that fits your organizational and company goals. Once you all agree to the "terms of engagement," communicate it far and wide.

Make sure you answer the following questions:

* How do SQA and documentation fit in with engineering?
* Who does marketing go to on the development team to resolve issues?
* Are all roles really well defined and well understood?

If you don't answer these basic questions, I guarantee that you and your teams will try to answer these questions at the start of every project. What a waste of time!

Team Basics

What is the optimum size of the development team? The size of teams is largely dependent on the following factors:

* Complexity of the project
* Length of time you have scheduled to deliver the project to market
* Experience the team has in building similar projects
* Your budget

It is assumed that your staff has all of the skills required to perform admirably. It is sometimes assumed that the more developers you have on a project, the faster the project will be completed. Nothing could be further from the truth!

Often, the more people you have on a project, the more communication and coordination is required. I like teams to be small—preferably less than 10 to 15 folks total. Some development managers claim that any headcount over eight is impossible to control and that the headcounts on a team must be odd (you know, 3, 5, 7) in order to "break ties" during heavy decision meetings.

If you operate in a consensus style and you believe in numerology (where certain combinations of numbers make sense and other combinations produce bad luck), then you are basing decisions on arbitrary factors.

Consensus-style management is bound to fail, in my experience. I have found it close to impossible for teams to come to 100-percent agreement on anything. Staffing projects to specific headcounts due to some theoretical study is just not relevant if your project may have many "loosely related" modules that need to be owned by different engineers.

The concept of reducing headcount as the project progresses is bound to appeal to upper management since it looks almost as if "the squeeze is being placed on the developers' heads—look at the productivity we're getting now!" Chances are the project had too large a headcount to begin with!

However, can you imagine how a team would feel if, the longer a project lasts, the fewer people are assigned to it? Not a pretty sight.

And how about the layers of development management required to handle all of the complex issues? The fewer the better—if you end up losing visibility into the project teams, you are too far removed from the action.

If you don't know the status of each team's progress, either team minutes are not getting properly circulated or, again, you are too far removed from the action.

Rules for the Unruly

Rule 58: Specify a responsible team headcount.

Here's a frequently asked question: "What should the ratio of SQA folks be to the number of engineers?" There is not one right answer, but you can make a few assumptions:

1. Your product must be a quality release (although the first release of a product may not be as thoroughly tested as one with thousands of customers).

2. Your product must have decent documentation to complement the product. Again, first releases may have minimal "niceties," such as simple on-line help or tutorials.

Now, does that help? Of course, the rules for what products should minimally include are pretty cut and dried. Quality testing does not constitute bringing in lots of temporaries who will "bang on the product"—I'm going to assume honest-to-goodness testers.

My experience is that the cost of documentation plus quality assurance should approximately equal the cost of engineering. So, if a project costs $1 million, then the cost breakdown would look something like Figure 4.3.

The cost for a project that is developed in a highly innovative state (with lots of engineering and experimentation) would be dramatically different. But, for the most part, if a project costs $1 million to produce, about $500,000 could be spent on engineering, with the remainder spent on documentation and quality assurance.

Rule 59: Match skills appropriately.

It is difficult to know if you have the right headcount and skills on the right project. Misjudging skills is a serious problem for development managers since you may be doing a disservice not only to the development employees but also to the company.

Rule 60: Reduce management hierarchies.

I like keeping as few manager levels as possible in development.

The organization chart in Figure 4.4 is an example of an engineering organization that has enough managers to "choke a pig."

Figure 4.3 Cost breakdown on an established project

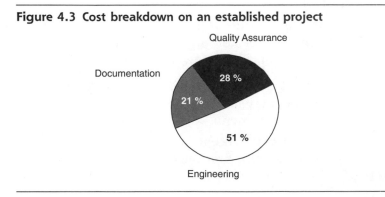

Figure 4.4 Typical software engineering manager hierarchy

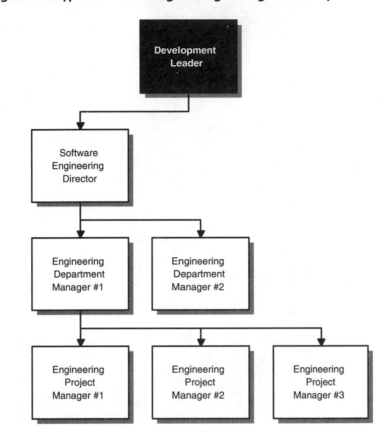

The organization represented in Figure 4.4 may be justified due to the project issues that always seem to surface, but if you find that the management headcount is a large percentage of headcount (in excess of 15 percent) and that the levels of communication take up a majority of management's time (through memos and meetings), you need to flatten the organization to something like the one shown in Figure 4.5.

How do you handle the additional responsibility when your organization expands—without building more management infrastructure? Easy:

1. Empower the team more.

Figure 4.5 Organization without excessive management hierarchies

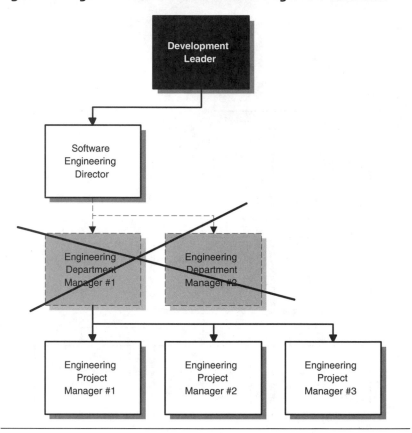

2. Don't do tasks that are unnecessary, and spend less time on tasks that will have only a minimal impact on the project (i.e., prioritize).

Rule 61: Make sure that team minutes are really being tracked.

The best way to communicate within development is not through endless status reports. Your job requires you to track and manage projects. Therefore you need to communicate the progress of the team in the form of regular team minutes.

So, what should team minutes entail? At a minimum, they should include the following topics:

• **Participants** There should be a list of who attended the meeting. The team should meet to talk mainly about project exceptions and tough issues. If key participants do not show up at the meeting, decisions cannot be made. I absolutely insist that if a key participant cannot attend, they provide a replacement who is "up to speed" enough to make decisions.

- **Issues resolved** Why not communicate key issues that have been resolved—there is nothing like experiencing success once in a while!

- **Outstanding issues left to be resolved** This list represents the dreaded action-item list. Each outstanding issue not resolved should be listed, with the name of the person (or persons) responsible and a due date for the issue to be resolved. If you can't make a decision, elevate the decision so that you get upper management's assistance.

- **Major project risks** Get the team to prioritize what they perceive are the biggest risks that could cause the project to either fail or to slip.

Make sure that the minutes are distributed within a couple of days of the actual meeting and make sure that the senior management receives a copy. If you sell internationally, do not forget to report to the international senior management!

Reality Checks

Check 31: Match people's skills to the correct job.

Rather than assume that you always have to hire additional people, are you sure that you have the right people assigned to the right tasks?

You wouldn't believe the number of times I've had this exchange with unprepared project managers:

"We need a programmer with experience in import filters for the next two months."

"Have you anyone in mind?"

"No, it will probably take a while to find a contractor or new hire."

"You know we have no additional budget and this certainly is a surprise request, given where we are on the project. When do you need the person?"

"Well, right now."

With further probing I usually find someone on the current staff who has the skills necessary. It would take some creative reassignments, but we could accommodate the change without additional headcount.

Any time you need some additional help and hiring has to occur, make every effort to find help from your current headcount. You cannot minimize the amount of effort it takes to hire while under pressure. Plus, you are almost guaranteed to miss schedules if this ad hoc hiring takes place during a project implementation.

One other alternative that you may not consider when you need more headcount: Look to your field consulting or sales organization for talent. Although these folks may not be able to program, there are usually some frustrated developers out there who would love the opportunity to temporarily work with development on their favorite project!

Practical Maniac Tips

Tip 23: Review the effectiveness of your organizational structure.

Chances are you'll be surprised by unseen hierarchies of management and processes that can slow projects to a crawl. You won't usually hear about these problem areas from your managers because the solutions might involve the elimination of some managerial positions!

Tip 24: Use team minutes effectively.

Are your team minutes really communicating the right issues? With your managers, define a format and content that all projects should use and get everyone on the same playing field.

I have found that the best-performing teams normally have the best quality and most timely team minutes.

Interesting Team Dynamics

There is always room for other leadership actions that help inspire your teams. I find myself being amused by teams that cycle between slow periods (rumors and idle talk commence) and fast periods (we're happy when we're busy).

Understanding these team dynamics is difficult for most development leaders, and development eventually assumes that development management is just "not in touch." The rules and case studies presented here will show an interesting alternative side to managing developers—one that you should keep in the back of your mind.

Rules for the Unruly

Rule 62: Keep the team interested by planning for the next revision.

Normally, projects take considerable time to plan and to implement. When a project takes months (or years) to complete, it's not unusual for the long hours to be spent at the "tail end" of a project. Burnout can easily occur when your teams start getting frustrated and even short tempered. I always like to start planning for the next revision of a product at the post-beta milestone.

In addition, some changes in pace can really help bolster morale, such as:

- Pizza-throwing parties (i.e., who has the funniest pizza design on their head?)
- Invite your neighborhood balloon man to learn something about each developer—a balloon will be fashioned for each personality
- Music night—everyone brings in their best and worst music, which is played over pizzas and beer (please treat Elvis with respect!)

    You get the idea!

Rule 63: Rank all of your employees based on performance.

As the development manager, you need to be able to find out who your top performers are at any given time. Here are some reasons:

- For pay (in other words, merit) increases
- In case of a layoff, you need to identify those who are not performing

- Identification of development's top performers who you can't afford to lose

In any case, I make it a habit—every 6 months—to prioritize performance of the entire development organization. And at each performance ranking session, I end up re-explaining the ranking system. To those being ranked, any uniform ranking system seems unworkable or unfair at first glance since each organization (engineering, SQA, and documentation) is so different.

Here are the steps:

1. Agree on job classifications that are the same across each organization. For example, classify development jobs into the following: entry level, advanced individual contributor, supervisor, manager, and designer.

   My managers then agree on where their specific job descriptions fall within each of these job classifications. As an example, *entry level* may include software engineer, SQA technician, and writer. *Supervisor* may include engineering project manager, SQA manager, and documentation manager. The point is to decide, as a group, what makes sense.

2. We all agree on a set of abilities at each job classification. Attached to each ability is a weight value from 1 to 10, where 1 means that an ability required for the job is of little value and 10 indicates the highest possible value. Table 4.1 is a partial table that I've used for three of the job classifications.

   As you can see, *entry level* does not require the developer to have high abstract reasoning, but this ability is strongly needed by advanced developers.

   By the way, we identify many other abilities as well—these three are just used to illustrate the ranking system.

Table 4.1 Assigning weights to abilities

Job Classification	Technical Ability	Abstract Reasoning	On Schedule Results	...
Entry Level	10	2	8	
Advanced	8	9	6	
Supervisor	7	5	10	

Table 4.2 Evaluating employees (entry level)

Entry Level [Engineers]	Technical Ability	Abstract Reasoning	On Schedule Results	...
John	5	3	4	
Mary	8	9	6	
...				

3. Each manager should perform an objective evaluation for each employee, using the ability guidelines previously agreed to by all managers. I'll show an example that evaluates four engineers. Ken and Timothy are advanced engineers, while John and Mary are entry-level engineers. It is every manager's initial view that Ken and Timothy will be the highest ranked engineers because they are the most experienced.

   Whenever you evaluate developers for their performance, you must evaluate them based on their value to their job level.

   Table 4.2 evaluates the two entry-level people, while Table 4.3 evaluates the advanced-level people.

4. Using Table 4.3, each manager can easily compute a weighted total. Given our sample four engineers, the ranking within the engineering group would look like Table 4.4.

Table 4.3 Evaluating employees (advanced level)

Advanced Level [Engineering]	Technical Ability	Abstract Reasoning	On Schedule Results	...
Ken	3	6	8	
Timothy	6	2	5	
...				

Table 4.4 Ranking of engineers

Engineering	Technical Ability	Abstract Reasoning	On Schedule Results	...	Total
Mary (entry)	8	9	6		146
Ken (advanced)	3	6	8		126
Timothy (advanced)	6	2	5		96
John (entry)	5	3	4		88
...					

Each developer's ability values are multiplied by their associated weight to produce a grand total. Notice that the resulting rankings show a good mix between entry-level and advanced engineers, with the top rated engineer, Mary, being a junior-level engineer.

At this point, each of your managers should have a good objective ranking of the people within their own department.

5. Now the fun really begins. All of the managers get together to determine which employees should be ranked the highest. As the development leader, you must be present to facilitate. This can be very difficult because some managers can get quite defensive, but the results are usually uncanny.

The top person on each manager's list is pitted against one another. As each manager presents his or her employee's strengths and weaknesses, a ranking list is created.

I've been able to facilitate a 50-person department ranking in approximately two hours!

Table 4.5 provides a sample ranking of developers. The dashed lines are used to separate the below-target, on-target, and above-target employees.

When your managers are not around, you will need to modify the ranking table to include them, too!

Table 4.5 Development's ranking

Developers	Department	Target
Mary (entry)	Engineering	Above
Nif (supervisor)	Documentation	Above
Mike (designer)	Documentation	Above
Ken (advanced)	Engineering	On
Debbie (designer)	Testing	On
Jaleh (advanced)	Documentation	On
Timothy (advanced)	Engineering	On
David (entry)	Documentation	On
John (entry)	Engineering	Below
Brian (supervisor)	Testing	Below
...	...	...

One important benefit of this method: By the time you have completed the department's evaluation, you have all learned a great deal about each other's employees.

Rule 64: Coach developers to help them make faster, well-informed decisions.

Teams can bog down when decision resolution just doesn't take place fast enough. Unfortunately, by the time management hears about the problem, frustration has probably spread through marketing and development.

If you stay informed by requesting and reading team minutes, you should have no trouble (provided the minutes are really representative of the team's true status) identifying projects that could use some help. In other words, if decisions are continually being postponed, you need to get involved.

Inform your project managers—in advance of team meetings—that you would like to help the team work through some key decisions. Surprising your managers by attending and taking over team meetings without any prior warning could seriously diminish their role with the teams.

At the team meeting, inform everyone of your intent and then help the team make the decisions.

Do not make decisions for the team.

If you do make decisions, you'll have to show up every week in order to continue making follow-up decisions.

Reality Checks

Check 32: Rank development.

When I began working with my managers to rank the entire department, the managers were really perplexed. They couldn't envision the benefits of the exercise. I encouraged them to forge ahead with the evaluations (you know, the "you're lucky to have a job" speech).

The ability evaluations went quickly and all of my managers were ready to compete. Each manager offered his or her top-evaluated employee and argued why this was or wasn't the department's best employee. The discussions were interesting and the engineering manager started:

"Mike is by far the most valuable employee to development. He single-handedly was responsible for the past two releases of our products. If I lost him to our competition, this company would be in big trouble. He has consistently been rewarded with large merit increases."

Next, the documentation manager:

"I think Mike is outstanding, but you should seriously consider Nif as the number one employee. She has written documentation the past three years that has reduced customer call volume and has actually won STC awards. I know that she is not an engineer, but her documentation has actually helped us win our two largest contracts last year."

Then the SQA manager:

"I think that Debbie is my best tester, by far. However, although she has demonstrated superior results the past six months, I consider both Nif and Mike to be better at their craft. If I can offer some advice, I believe that Mike is more critical to our department and his job because all of our people depend on him for counseling."

And on it goes until the list of employees is exhausted. In this case, the documentation group demonstrated themselves to be the best managed and the most talented of all my groups. Six months later, SQA was the highest ranked group. The SQA manager took to heart the feedback that the engineering and documentation managers communicated about his staff during the ranking meeting.

Practical Maniac Tips

Tip 25: Rank development and help your managers work as one management team.

Take your development organization through the ranking exercise described in Rule 63. The first time you work through this exercise, you might find it to be rough going. Share the results with your personnel representative if it makes sense to do so. It's also a great idea to discuss the performance ranking of your folks with your boss.

There is a potential risk, though. If the results show that your organization is not very highly ranked (i.e., on target instead of above target in performance), your group's performance basically reflects *your* performance! Get it?

In Summary

Place development organizations on an equal footing.

Even though the engineering organization may have the highest perceived value to the organization, make sure that all development groups share the load and the responsibility. The term "development" implies *all* the development disciplines—including engineering, testing, and documentation.

Keep teams small and effective.

Although there is no rule of thumb to identify ideal headcount, one rule does tend to work: the smaller the teams, the better the teams.

Remove layers of management.

The complexity of modern-day software development really justifies detail-driven management. You know you have too many layers of management if you have no exposure to individual developers.

Team minutes are the most important status-update tool you can use.

Of the mounds of memos and status reports I receive regularly, most of my attention becomes focused on project team minutes that review critical issues affecting a project's eventual delivery to market. My ultimate goal is to reduce all non-team minute memos by 90 percent!

Plan early for next releases.

Don't wait for a project to ship to market before you start thinking about the next version. When you reach a key milestone on a project (preferably alpha or beta test), start planning for the next version.

Rank your development organization.

I've shown you one way to objectively performance-rank all of development using a single list. Whatever technique you use, make sure that it is fair and objective. If you still can't figure out why you should rank employees, look back at the bulleted list in Rule 63.

Schedules

A software project always executes better when a process is associated with it—as long as everyone is accountable and knows what schedule milestones require. If handled properly, schedule leadership can be a "motivator" rather than a "threat to creativity."

This chapter focuses on what it takes to properly handle schedules, including:

- Simple schedule milestones
- Roles and responsibilities
- Who determines when a milestone has been met
- Who communicates the schedules

Simple Schedule Milestone Definitions

A product calendar is a summary of schedules of projects under development. Project progress needs to be measured against key points of accomplishment (the milestone).

Schedules need to be more detailed than just *start* and *release*. It's necessary to use milestones that satisfy the following basic criteria. Milestones should:

- Be easy to understand.
- Provide a way to validate major achievements.
- Provide value to your organization so that everyone will know their role.
- Include an objective set of guidelines for both marketing and development.
- Help determine whether a project is on schedule.

Of course, all of the above criteria is positive and tends to justify milestone usage. Unfortunately, many people perceive milestones in a negative way. To some developers, milestones:

- Mean little to the results of the company.
- Discourage the creativity required to develop best-of-breed products.
- Force "sandbagging" of projects that could be released sooner.

The list could go on and on. When milestones are developed and used correctly, none of these negative perceptions about milestones will have any truth, but if you let the schedule milestone process drive decisions, some of the negatives may be justified.

Milestones and associated roles should be only a "barometer" to help management determine a project's status at any time and should help keep the project team focused on attaining interim checkpoints.

And that's *all* they should be.

I've heard statements made like:

"Our milestone process helps us meet schedules."

That is simply not true. The fact that a process is in place doesn't mean that project delivery dates will meet schedules. The milestone process is a set of passive guidelines on a piece of paper. The team and management must use the milestone process as an aid to identify risks and major issues that constantly "pop up" at all stages of a project.

What's the most important criterion for milestones? Make them simple! How simple? Read on.

Table 5.1 shows a set of milestone definitions that I have used successfully for years. I could spend chapters discussing what needs to be accomplished at each milestone. But Table 5.1 should provide you with enough guidance to help you create your own milestone definitions.

Table 5.1 Milestone definitions

Milestone	*Simple Definition*
Concept	Marketing presents the idea to executive management in order to gain funding approval—development management is made aware of the concept in advance.
Proposal	Marketing and development managers jointly prepare a business plan or executive review. This could present a product's scope, competitive outlook, pro forma of revenue and profit, and rough schedule.
Specification	Development produces prototypes from marketing's "storyboards" and completes specifications and user interface testing. Marketing signs off—the plans must match what marketing originally expected the project to accomplish.
Alpha	Product is functionally complete—but probably crashes quite a lot. At this point, internal users (within the company) can start using the product, and test plans and documentation can now be written.
Beta	Product passes rudimentary tests, which uncover no crashes and determine that the product is functionally complete;

continued

Table 5.1 Milestone definitions (continued)

Milestone	Simple Definition
	also, draft documentation is ready for review. The product is available for external (customer) beta testing. For products that are or will be multilingual (i.e., can be translated), now is the time to start performing some sample translations.
Release	Testing has been completed and the product is shipped. Congratulations.
Post mortem	The team reassembles and hashes out what went well and what went poorly. At the same time, the product (and all its components) are archived.

 Rules for the Unruly

Rule 65: Make milestones simple and usable.

Whatever milestones you decide to use, make them simple to comprehend and administrate. If milestones are too ambiguous and do not serve as an effective barometer that you can use to evaluate the project in a way that leads ultimately to successful project delivery, you had better redefine them.

Rule 66: Construct delivery schedules that represent what you know.

Look at the schedule in Table 5.2. Does anything look strange?

This project is scheduled for approximately one year and includes specific dates. You will be under a lot of pressure to fill in all or most milestones at this level of detail. But you usually will not have enough information at the start of a project to create a reliable schedule that includes dates for *every* milestone.

The schedule shown in Table 5.3 can produce the same results and yet is more credible.

Do you see why this schedule is more credible? As each milestone is achieved (I like to highlight milestones accomplished

---

Table 5.2 Sample schedule of milestones in product calendar (not recommended)

Project	Concept	Proposal	Spec	Alpha	Beta	Release	Post-mortem
Jason	Aug 10	Sept 5	Dec 18	Mar 15	July 30	Aug 5	Sep 1

Table 5.3 Sample schedule of milestones (better)

Project	Concept	Proposal	Spec	Alpha	Beta	Release	Post-mortem
Jason	Aug 10	Sept 5	Dec	Q1	Q3	Q3	Q3/4

Table 5.4 Milestone dates after concept and proposal have been achieved

Project	Concept	Proposal	Spec	Alpha	Beta	Release	Post-mortem
Jason	Aug 10	Sept 3	Dec 15	Mar	Q3	Q3	Q3/4

in our product calendars), subsequent milestones become more refined, as shown in Table 5.4.

What does the original schedule (Table 5.2) mean to your CFO? Plenty. The CFO will start planning revenue in the quarter following the release (in this case, fourth quarter).

Rule 67: If one milestone slips, so will the others.

Let's say that your alpha milestone slips one month past the point you had originally scheduled. Your project manager tells you, "Don't worry, we'll make it up at beta." You can either:

1. believe her

or

2. insist she digest the following paragraph:

   You *rarely* make up schedules when an earlier schedule milestone slips past the target date. Either move the rest of the scheduled dates back in accordance with your current slip or reduce functionality in order to try to meet the original schedule. The term "rarely" in development means "never."

Rule 68: Track schedule dependencies/risks by using a product calendar.

A product calendar is used to keep track of all project schedules. For each project being tracked, make sure that you address the major risks associated with attaining the next milestone.

Consider an example. To achieve the alpha milestone of a specific project (call it Jason), the most critical risk could be identified in the product calendar as shown in Table 5.5.

Table 5.5 Excerpt of a product calendar

Project	Milestone	Major risk/issue
Jason	Alpha	The graphics engine functional requirements need to be resolved between marketing and development by the 15th of March.

In fact, when risks associated with any project become reality, the project becomes instantly visible to executive management—to the point where resolution of that risk becomes everyone's concern! By identifying risks for each milestone in advance, you can track the project to ensure that risks either don't become reality or can be resolved before they draw the wrath of executive management. (Note that the product calendar excerpt in Table 5.5 should be combined with the information shown earlier, starting with the example shown in Table 5.2. We just ran out of column width in this book to combine them into one table!)

Rule 69: There is little difference between new and updated projects.

What do you do about schedules that are only updates of previous projects? Should you implement the same schedule detail you would normally develop for new projects? Or do milestones need to be redefined for projects that are just updates?

This question stumps a lot of development groups. Development is typically not sure what to do in this situation, and marketing will often want to skip any and all milestones on product updates!

Do not invent an alternative milestone process for product updates—you don't need to!

Let the team agree at the beginning of an update project whether any milestones are to be ignored. Better yet, combine milestones in order to speed the process along, but still show that the process can fit most any project. A technique that has worked for me is to combine the concept and proposal milestones for product updates.

Reality Checks

Check 33: What do you do with the "Milestone Bible?"

Determining which milestones to use is a difficult task. I've seen numerous occasions where senior development and marketing management spend months constructing a "milestone bible" (commonly known as the product development process). This monster paperweight has every task, every signoff, every form, and every definition known to man (and woman) to help project team members manage the tasks of basic milestone administration. There are tons of reference books that try to educate us on the "development process"—most are sadly outdated.

If your milestone guidelines are so detailed that you need full-time program managers just to administer them, you've defined milestones that are unnecessarily complex. (By the way, program managers are typically called "seagulls" by developers, because their job is to go around and dump you-know-what on everyone on a project team.)

My development groups have agreed on this milestone-definition process, with the following steps listed in Table 5.6.

Okay—so it takes a grand total of 15 hours to agree on milestones. Sounds excessive? Well, this entire milestone definition had gained complete agreement in approximately two

Table 5.6 Agreement of product delivery milestones

Step	Time	Description
1	2 hours	Development and marketing managers agree on the basic milestones.
2	5 hours (pizza required)	Development and marketing management meet with project managers to agree on roles at each milestone. See "Roles and Responsibilities" later in this chapter.
3	2 hours (I gotta have the chart in order to look good)	I create a chart that shows each milestone activity for any project.
4	4 hours	Get everyone in development to buy into the milestones (this includes the engineers, writers, and testers). Why just development? In all honesty, these people perform most of the activities in project delivery.

continued

Table 5.6 Agreement of product delivery milestones (continued)

Step	Time	Description
5	2 hours	Get all managers of each organization (marketing, development, sales, distribution, customer support, and finance) together to review each milestone's definition and everyone's role at each milestone.
Total	15 hours	Milestone definitions complete!

working days. We may have saved months of the needless negotiation, which would have resulted if we had just left the various groups alone to "fight among themselves" how to define the process.

Practical Maniac Tips

Tip 26: Jointly complete the product calendar.

Once you agree on project milestones, you, development, and marketing managers should meet to jointly fill out your complete product calendar. Don't forget to include each project's major risks or issues that could affect attainment of the next milestone.

Tip 27: Keep project records.

Start a project workbook. All specifications, documents, and monthly schedules should be put into this binder. In one sense, this binder becomes the official history of the project.

Roles and Responsibilities

So, you've created an outstanding milestone process, and the goals of each milestone are pretty clear. But you're still going to hear a lot of grumbling and you'll have to resolve a lot of problems if you don't determine *who* is responsible for *which goals* in the milestone process.

At each milestone, team members may have problems with the following:

• Who should be a part of the team at this specific milestone?

- What is everyone's role at each milestone?
- Who is responsible for making sure milestones are really achieved?

Rules for the Unruly

Rule 70: Decide who is involved at each milestone.

The easiest approach to creating a team environment is to have everyone on the team attend all team meetings and participate at each milestone. This may make sense for small projects. But for most of us, it is far wiser to use people at key milestones only when needed. Junior project development managers wishing to show "team drive" will quickly get bogged down trying to satisfy everyone's demands throughout the project's activities if everyone is always involved.

The more experienced manager will sit down with the entire team at the beginning of a project and review the milestones. At each milestone, the manager should facilitate a discussion where people's roles are identified. An example would be:

"Customer support has little involvement at the alpha milestone; however, three weeks before beta we will need regular customer support attendance at our meetings. In fact for this project, beta won't be achieved until customer support is trained on the features of the product."

Rule 71: Use an appropriate tool to track the product calendar.

Don't waste valuable time managing project management software instead of your project. Some tremendous project scheduling tools are available to help you track schedules. Most of them, however, are overkill, unless you have a tremendous number of dependencies between components of the project.

I constantly revert to a simple word processor or spreadsheet to keep track of the product calendar.

Rule 72: Make sure that everyone's role is clear.

It is not enough to have clear milestone definitions if folks on the team (or those outside of the team) do not comprehend what everyone should be doing at each milestone. See Reality Check 34 for more details on assigning roles to ensure that milestones are met.

🌀 Reality Checks

Check 34: Define everyone's role.

Using the beta milestone from Table 5.1, Table 5.7 shows how we defined each organization's role. I've used this completed milestone chart (Table 5.7) ever since.

Table 5.7 Beta milestone's roles and responsibilities

Organization	*Role and Responsibility*
Executive Management	Informed via electronic mail (sent from marketing product manager) that milestone had been achieved. No specific action required.
Product Marketing	Reports to wide distribution list that beta has been achieved, releases press statements, and begins product-launch preparation. Marketing prepares to demonstrate product to sales.
Engineering	Engineering has produced a product that is fully functional with no known crashing bugs.
Quality Assurance (QA)	Quality assurance has passed the engineering beta version with complete execution of its current test plan. QA installs and trains customer support and training with the beta software immediately.
Documentation	Documentation has released the draft user's manual along with base training material and on-line help. All other team members have approximately two weeks to review the documentation for correctness.
Customer Support	Customer receives the beta software and training. Prepares for customer support by calling customers in advance of their receiving the beta software.
Training	The training for beta begins. Training curriculum is now being reviewed, and classes are being scheduled to coincide with the product launch.
Distribution (or Fulfillment)	Sends the beta media out for duplication and prepares the beta packages for shipment both to external customers and internal employees.
Sales	Receives beta training from marketing on the new product and starts preparing how to handle customer penetration.

Check 35: Use this milestone team building exercise.

Figure 5.1 shows a potential problem situation where team members may not agree that the alpha milestone had been properly achieved.

Unless you spend the time getting your managers to know how to handle milestone conflicts, you'll be spending a lot of time refereeing situation after situation. I have used the worksheet in Figure 5.1 as a guide to resolve milestone conflicts by adhering to three basic steps:

1. Restate the problem (or situation).
2. Agree on the goal you all wish to achieve once the problem is solved.
3. Facilitate (don't dictate) your managers through the "team building approach."

Figure 5.1 Solving a milestone problem

ALPHA MILESTONE

Problem/Situation

"We all know what our respective roles are at the alpha milestone, but quality assurance and documentation do not agree with engineering that alpha has been achieved. And marketing thinks we're about ready to ship! What's a manager to do?"

Goal

To develop creative ideas that will help development managers resolve this situation.

TEAM BUILDING APPROACH

Create the problem solving team. Break managers into cross-discipline (composed of engineering, quality assurance, support, etc.) teams. Have one manager facilitate.

Define the problem. Give this team the Milestone and the Problem/Situation— ask for questions or elaboration so that everyone is clear what the problem is.

Examples always help. Allow the team to present examples of personal experiences that relate to the problem. The facilitator writes down the key points.

Brainstorming. Facilitator will write down ideas. Then, the team should prioritize the ideas based on how useful they will be in solving the problem. Ideas should not be "destroyed" while brainstorming is taking place; otherwise, some team members might just shut down and tune out.

Presentation. To get the ideas out in the open, the team gets back together and the facilitator presents the prioritized ideas to all of the managers. The ideas, plus background explanations, can really be beneficial to all of the managers.

In this example, we finally agreed that for the good of the customer, if quality assurance and documentation do not consent to alpha milestone being met, then the alpha milestone is simply not yet achieved!

 ## Practical Maniac Tips

Tip 28: Practice resolving milestone situations with your management team.

Use the sample milestone worksheet in Figure 5.1 as a blueprint to create your organization's roles and responsibilities at each milestone.

Practice defining a similar milestone worksheet with your managers first, as a "dry run." You don't need expensive consultants to help facilitate this activity since you, as the development leader, ought to be able to facilitate this exercise.

Determining when a Milestone Has Been Met

This is one of the most difficult points in milestone management. How in the world do you determine whether a schedule has been achieved?

The best way to answer this question is through a case study. First, though, consider some basic rules.

Rules for the Unruly

Rule 73: Don't forget to refine subsequent schedule milestones.

Once you agree that a milestone has been achieved, the team ought to refine the remaining milestones left in the project schedule. See the examples in Tables 5.3, 5.4, and 5.5.

Rule 74: Don't "force fit" a milestone.

Just because you *want* to achieve a milestone, it doesn't automatically follow that the milestone will successfully *be* achieved.

It is the responsibility of your team leader (normally, the product marketing manager) to listen to the team's recommendation and to acknowledge milestone attainment.

I've forced a schedule re-evaluation when it appears that a major milestone attainment has been forced.

Reality Checks

Check 36: What if all milestones don't come together?

Often, a project will achieve a milestone in different stages. For example, a database project composed of three major modules may achieve alpha at different points, as illustrated in Figure 5.2.

In Figure 5.2, as individual modules (1, 2, 3, ...) are achieving alpha at different times, what date should you use to specify completion? When all three modules achieve alpha or when two of the three modules achieve alpha?

Although the precise answer depends on the specific project you are working on, the team must agree that a milestone is met when certain basic requirements have been achieved. Agreement on a milestone's completion date must give the team confidence that the next milestone can be met.

For instance, the team may agree that alpha is met when modules 1 and 2 are complete and the user interface of module 3 is complete. The fact that all of the components of module 3 may not be at a "true alpha" may not adversely affect the team's ability to judge whether alpha is achieved. Some product components don't make alpha until a week before beta! With some

---

Figure 5.2 Achieving alpha

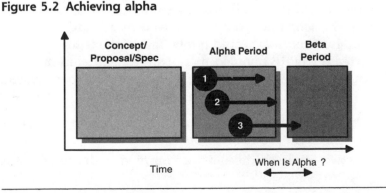

technologies, alpha quality can't be achieved until some components are at a near-beta condition.

I can think of one example. When a desktop publishing product (or word processor, for that matter) is being developed, the text engine that handles all of the layout and font dimensions must be at near-beta quality before any of the other functions (search and replace, style sheets, etc.) can achieve alpha status.

Check 37: Elevate schedule conflicts.

Pay attention to this one.

Engineering says, "Our beta milestone has been achieved." Quality assurance (the testing group) says, "There is no way this project made beta!" Who's right?

Although I tend to trust what the testers say, this particular situation isn't quite that simple to solve.

Rather than let the team members "slug it out" among themselves and suffer the consequences (which are usually that certain team members will no longer talk to each other), the engineering project leader and the product manager should elevate the issue to their managers. This approach gets senior management involved in facilitating a resolution for what typically can be a very emotional issue among team members.

This strategy also removes some of the pressure that the two managers may face between themselves and the team. I'll never forget one unpleasant situation, where the development team was asked to add a feature that had been intentionally removed (via another request) at the beginning of the project.

We were two weeks from beta, and this change would adversely affect the schedule by approximately two weeks. If the request could not be absorbed within the current schedule, adjusting the schedule would be viewed by management as a schedule slip. And that would not be fair to the team.

The team (rightly) hauled me into the next team meeting, and we decided to elevate the issue to the executive management team on Monday. The executive team heard two alternatives:

1. Stick to the original schedule and add the requested feature in a subsequent product update.
2. Take a two-week schedule hit to accommodate the new feature.

The team recommended moving the schedule back two weeks to accommodate the feature, since there was potential customer impact. The executive team agreed and the schedule was *adjusted* so that development would not be perceived as having slipped.

Practical Maniac Tips

Tip 29: Take the opportunity to teach your teams how to resolve milestone conflicts.

Although you don't want to embarrass a specific team, try to isolate a specific, difficult schedule decision for use as an example. When a specific project's milestone attainment required a creative resolution (which, of course, is the difficult schedule decision), you may wish to discuss the circumstances and outcome with the entire cast of marketing and development managers.

Milestone conflict resolution just won't "sink in" without real-life examples!

Who Communicates Schedules?

Who do you appoint within the organization to communicate schedules? You should assign a single contact person—the marketing product manager—who will announce schedules and report their progress to all of the organizations involved. I continually find the reason a schedule slips is that individual roles and responsibilities (I really mean "accountability") are not clear.

Rules for the Unruly

Rule 75: Adjust milestone definitions if you need more milestones.

There are many cases where your project may need more milestones than the basic implementation set: alpha and beta. You may need an alpha 1, alpha 2, alpha 3, and so on. Rather than redefine your entire milestone system and report a different set of milestones for each project, let the team micro manage the additional interim milestones, but still report only on the major milestones for consistency.

A VP of sales can't keep up with different milestone definitions for each project—in fact, he or she may think that development is trying to fool the sales organization with varied definitions of progress!

Rule 76: The product calendar audience should be fairly wide.

Who should have access to the product calendar? Here's a list of folks I believe should have regular access to milestone information:

- President or CEO
- CFO
- VP of sales (U.S. and/or international)
- All product managers
- All development managers
- Customer support manager
- Training manager
- Marketing communication (MARCOM)

Don't be afraid to keep these schedules confidential. If customers get hold of them, you run the risk of this information getting to your competitors.

Rule 77: Projects usually have legal responsibilities.

Your company may have legal and even contractual obligations to keep archives of your product technologies off-site. After a product is released, the product *must* be properly archived, preferably off-site at some safe location.

You may need to re-create a product months or even years after it is released. *Protect yourself!*

A project should *never* be removed from the product calendar until it has been properly archived and proven that it can be rebuilt on a "virgin" system. I can't recall the number of times my development groups believed they could re-create a product when, in reality, doing so was impossible simply because some key files had not been saved properly.

Reality Checks

Check 38: The one who leads the team, owns the schedule.

In this situation no marketing person had been hired, so development led all project team meetings. The engineering project manager took on the role of overall team leader. With some careful coaching on my part, this approach was pretty successful.

Project managers who had problems "working" the team to closure were removed from those roles (so were those who *forced* teams to closure). Bringing a team to closure on issues requires leadership yet still requires that the leader listen to contrary opinions from normally very disobedient development team members.

One of our biggest problems was deciding how to transition teams once the marketing folks came on board. We didn't want to wait for marketing to force the team ownership issue. We wanted to make sure the transition would take place smoothly.

These are the steps we took to properly transition product management responsibilities from development to marketing:

1. We assured the project managers that their role leading teams had, to date, been successful. However, the product launch and coordination issues were simply not being handled effectively and these issues could easily take time out of the project managers' daily routine.

2. We worked on a "transition plan" that was communicated to the team at a meeting jointly led by the product and project managers. I attended this particular meeting just to make sure that everything went well. It did.

3. From this point on, the product marketing manager took control of the team meeting and authored the team minutes. The development team set up its own preparatory meeting to anticipate issues before each team meeting.

Check 39: "Oops, we forgot to get schedule buy-in!"

A problem that I constantly run across is a failure to get team buy-in at the early (concept and proposal milestones) stages of a project. Marketing feels that there is not enough time to do so or that there is no need to involve the development organization.

It is not unusual to receive a sample concept document that the development project managers hadn't ever seen or even heard about. If this surprise happens to you, immediately hand over the document to your development managers and have them work out the details with their marketing counterpart.

If they can't agree on basic concepts, then issues should be elevated to senior management to resolve. This situation would not have even taken place if the proper buy-in with development had occurred.

Practical Maniac Tips

Tip 30: Use a schedule worksheet to track key development issues.

Even though marketing should communicate an overall corporate product calendar, you will need to make sure that milestones are being properly represented. Your development organization should maintain its own schedule worksheet, with enough detail to track key development issues associated with every project under development. This schedule will need to be coordinated with marketing before the "official" product calendar is distributed.

Make schedule issues a permanent agenda item in your regular development management meetings.

In Summary

Make milestones simple and usable.

Whatever milestones you decide to use, make them simple to comprehend and make sure they are usable.

Make sure that everyone's role is clear.

It is not enough to have clear milestone definitions if folks on the team (or those outside of the team) do not comprehend what everyone should be doing at each milestone.

Don't force-fit a milestone to accommodate "wanna be" schedules.

It is tempting to say that a schedule milestone has been attained when, in reality, it hasn't.

Let marketing own the schedule communication.

Although you may be tempted to completely own schedule management and communication, product marketing really is responsible.

If a milestone is gonna slip . . . .

Don't just absorb it. Develop alternatives that will either return the project to the schedule or justify the slip. You can always put a project back on schedule by reducing product content (as long as that move doesn't affect market share or customer expectations).

Don't ever plan for milestones to be achieved at the end of a financial period.

Simply stated, if you need to release a product in the fourth quarter (usually October through December), do not proclaim a Q4 delivery date if your best guess schedule release is late December. If that is the case, you've really given the company a Q1 (or next quarter) schedule!

Office Dynamics

Do you believe cubicles work for your employees? Forget it! Even though companies today often recommend the cubicle work environment, I believe I can easily prove them wrong. By the way, productivity is more important than office aesthetics—never forget that you're paying people to be productive.

This chapter will challenge you and your company to be more productive, but it will allow you to do so at only a minimal cost, and by using a large dose of common sense. Topics include:

- Creating an effective work environment
- Offices versus cubicles
- Working at home (is there a problem?)

Creating an Effective Work Environment

A chair, desk, light, and a computer—who could ask for more? Cubicles for open atmosphere, meetings once a week. Hell, your people must be in absolute heaven.

Well, not quite.

How restrictive is the dress code? Is overtime the rule, not the exception? And why does it seem like developers aren't doing anything half the time?

Rules for the Unruly

Rule 78: Identify the environmental factors that stifle development's productivity.

Why be content with your current office environment? Chances are your organization has some problems that can be easily corrected (and for little money). Even if you can't solve all of the problems, you can at least identify what the problems are.

Rule 79: Improve your office productivity issues creatively and inexpensively.

There are probably many situations where you can solve productivity issues creatively. For example, we found that the intercom system was being heavily used to "page" employees. These announcements seemed important, but they were very distracting. We could expect to hear someone being paged about once every five minutes. And it seemed ridiculous to use intercom paging when everyone had personal voice mail messaging systems.

As soon as I realized this was a disruption, I asked the senior staff if they were willing to nuke "pages" completely (except, of course, for genuine emergencies). They all approved the idea, although a couple of folks were hesitant about doing so.

Well, the decision worked. The receptionists were thrilled. They no longer had to spend valuable time trying to locate people who weren't at their desks. Instead of frequent announcements like "Ms. B, Mr. G is waiting at some airport," the office became pleasantly quiet. And how much did this change cost the company? Since everyone already had voice mail and electronic mail, the cost was nothing.

Reality Checks

Check 40: Developers need an environment that allows them to be productive.

Just because your developers receive competitive salaries, you can't assume they'll be content, productive, and motivated. With development, you also must offer a competitive work environment. Here is my basic checklist:

- Satisfactory office arrangement (see "Offices versus Cubicles" later in this chapter)
- Access to LAN and centralized network services
- Decent computer system with high resolution video display
- Legal copies of all software tools necessary to perform job duties
- Available meeting space

In our building, we could not provide an office arrangement that was totally conducive to the above checklist. However, we outgrew our building and in planning our new building's office arrangements, we were able to accommodate the following in the office design:

- Private offices
- Plenty of meeting space
- Covered parking with 24-hour security
- Ability to take advantage of twisted-pair, high-speed LAN wiring (built into the office walls!)

Check 41: Developers should not be the only productive group.

The list in Reality Check 40 specifies some simple requirements that can help *developers* be more productive. But what about customer support, sales, and other organizations?

Other organizations within a software company often felt that development's work environment was better than theirs. Whenever this perception occurred, I immediately went on a campaign to encourage my peers (in other organizations) to improve their office environments to the same level as development enjoyed—or at least to bring their office environments into the 1990s!

And you can help!

Small gestures can get big results. For instance, each Friday, it was customary to bring in donuts for the development group. We decided to expand the delivery to include *all* groups in the company. Wow, talk about instant togetherness!

Here's another example. For development meetings, it was common practice to bring in food (such as pizza). In fact, our slogan was: "We don't meet unless we eat!"

When development is consolidated with non-development employees in one building, dress codes can clash. It was not unusual for our developers to work in shorts and tee shirts. Non-developers never dressed that casually (except when the company designated special "dress down days").

Well, rather than provide a rear entrance for the developers, we made two more productive changes:

1. Non-developers could dress down to business casual attire which, unless employees would be entertaining a customer, meant nice slacks and dresses. Designer dresses and suits became a thing of the past. In fact, this policy actually helped promote a change in company culture: When people at different levels within the company dress alike, they tend to act more like peers. The culture quickly went from bureaucracy to one of empowerment without useless concern of attire.

2. Developers would, in turn, dress *up* to business casual (as well as they were able, since developers tend to be "wardrobe challenged"). For them, tee shirts, blue jeans, and tennis shoes became things of the past.

Perhaps you're thinking, "There is no way I could enforce that kind of dress code with our folks!" Think again. A company needs to present a uniform culture in order to encourage harmony among organizations. If you're in danger of losing key employees simply because they don't want to be subjected to "dress codes," chances are you're going to lose them for some *other* reason. If key people do threaten to quit over a dress code, you might be able to change their minds by pointing out that their next job will probably be with a company that also enforces a dress code—and possibly a more severe one! In any case, when you announce the new dress code policy, reassure everyone that they won't have to purchase a new wardrobe. Handle the transition to more business-casual attire sensibly.

Check 42: Red Light, Green Light

My development managers and I determined that productivity was being negatively affected by excessive noise in the office. Part of the problem stemmed from the fact that developers were forced to work in cubicles. I hadn't yet been able to convince executive management that developers needed to be in separate offices. In addition to the noise, developers complained that their concentration was frequently disrupted by people who would wander into their cubes to talk about some business or personal matter. There were just too many interruptions each day!

What to do?

We gathered everyone in development together to decide how to handle our little problem. We talked about various ways to control the noise and decided on a unique solution: We would signal each other in a way that would indicate our level of concentration and our availability, but that would not be taken negatively. Developers tend to need long periods of time to concentrate—and that means no interruptions.

We decided on a set of simple " traffic signals" that could be hung outside of everyone's cubicles to control the noise and interruptions. Here's what each signal means:

- **Red light:** "Do not enter. I'm extremely busy."
- **Yellow light:** "Enter only in case of emergencies."

- **Green light:** "Come on in. I'm busy, but available to communicate."

As a fun exercise, everyone in development created his or her own lights out of construction paper during lunch—management supplied the food and drinks. In addition, I let marketing know about our idea, since I realized they might view it as childish and unprofessional. They didn't—they thought the idea was great! Will wonders never cease . . . .

We did enforce one major rule. Can you imagine what that was?

If someone always keeps the red light on, chances are you have a person that is not much of a team player. You need to ensure that this system is sensibly used, not abused.

In a little over two hours, we successfully solved what had appeared to everyone to be a major productivity problem. And all it cost was some food, drinks, and construction paper.

Practical Maniac Tips

Tip 31: Use your managers to improve office productivity.

Rather than wait for changes to take place due to "executive management resolutions," why not meet with your personnel organization to address issues that affect your office work environment? Set up a task force composed of both development managers and individual contributors. The goal is to review the basic issues that affect your work environment. I guarantee that problems will become apparent and may even surprise you.

Offices Versus Cubicles

The top 10 reasons why managers believe cubicles work for modern-day software development:

1. They're cheaper than offices to maintain.
2. They represent the ultimate in fashion.
3. They foster communication.
4. Cubicles have been proven to use space efficiently.
5. Cubicles inspire teamwork.

6. Management needs to be able look over the floor and see the activities that are taking place.

7. The use of cubicles matches what our customers use—we would find it unacceptable to have a more private work atmosphere than our customers have.

8. Cubicles will cut down on the "I want to work at home for the next few days so that I can get some work done" requests.

9. Cubicles help us get to know each other personally and help us develop an appreciation for each other's musical tastes.

10. There is no choice but to accept cubicles as the corporate standard.

Whew! Some of the reasons sound kind of foolish, right? Not so. I've heard them all (and I bet you have, too).

Now that you've read through the top 10 list of cubicle misconceptions, take a look at the top 10 hints that suggest you may have a major productivity problem brewing:

1. You hear frequent complaints that "noise" is preventing people from getting things done.

2. There are too many ad hoc hallway conversations.

3. Developers ask to work at home for a few days in order to "get some work done."

4. Employees know more about other developers' families than they do about their own.

5. You notice that developers shift their working hours to out-of-the-norm hours (even against their personal preferences).

6. You find that schedules are constantly not being met—there may be a problem with developers' ability to concentrate when periods of non-disruption are few and far between.

7. Because some developers listen to music as they work (I do—I've done loud budgets to the music of Prince, Peter Gabriel, and George Strait), headphone "bleed" can disrupt others.

8. Telephones constantly ring from neighboring cubicles.

9. Developers find themselves more often in conference rooms to escape their cubicles (or open work areas).

10. You fill in this one!

Although a couple of the above hints are not entirely serious, their overall intent is: I believe that most developers do not know the full impact of office environment on productivity because they've never been exposed to better office arrangements.

Rules for the Unruly

Rule 80: Offices are better than cubicles and cubicles are better than open work areas.

I hate open work areas where several desks are in a large room. I've seen them too many times—especially in Japan. This setup does offer an environment where everyone can keep tabs on each other. But for developers, it is just plain nuts.

You already know how I feel about cubicles. I hope that, if you didn't feel the same before you began this chapter, you do now! Do something about it! For instance, at the top of cubicles, put in planters with vines that will quickly grow to the ceiling. I'm not kidding—it helps!

Rule 81: Even if you have cubicles, do something better.

OK, so it's unrealistic to change your company to offices. How about rearranging the entrances to the cubicles in a way that diverts traffic? Or how about muffling all phones? You can take some interesting and creative steps to improve productivity.

Reality Checks

Check 43: Take office productivity into your own hands.

Sometimes a move to a new building can be just the ticket to resolve office-arrangement problems. Chances are you have a facilities person (or organization) who has strict rules from "el presidente" that forbids the use of offices.

I've had the same thing pulled on me.

So, I immediately requested an office that would be smaller than I was allowed in the new office space. Right. Now you got the facilities guy's attention.

.I then flooded the facilities organization with facts about office productivity. Note Tim Lister's book *Peopleware*, is an outstanding source. Then I presented real proof. I called several of the key proponents of office productivity: Microsoft, Apple, and Data General. And I wrote down actual quotations. (If that fails, invent your own statistics!)

Next, the ultimate: Every company has guidelines of square footage per employee; you are expected to accommodate space for your folks that matches that guideline. How can you do it? Well, these two approaches often work:

1. If necessary, justify having two developers share an office—this approach, although not optimum, will dramatically reduce the square feet per employee.

2. Find a source that can beat the price of the designer cubicle furniture and walls your facilities guy was going to recommend. Although you can depreciate office furniture over a long period of time, I guarantee that if you search, there are ways to construct walls in a cost effective manner.

   I've seen so-called "industry giants" (even those with development background) indicate that cubicles are the only way to go. These are the same people who preach that teams should only have specific headcounts (some small odd number). Don't believe it!

Practical Maniac Tips

Tip 32: Prove to management that office arrangements and policy will affect people's productivity.

Buy your management team *Managing Software Maniacs* if you all agree with the reasons to switch to offices. Buy additional copies for all of senior management and highlight those pages you want them to read.

You must be extremely careful how you communicate your ability to solve office (versus cubicles) arrangements to developers, because you may get their hopes up without being able to follow through on private offices.

Working at Home

Remember the situation I mentioned earlier where developers ask to work at home in order to get some work done? Well, what do you do if developers want to work at home?

I can predict with absolute certainty that entire teams of engineers will eventually be working at home and basically telecommuting with their co-workers over the phone (including video conferencing), via bulletin boards, or through electronic mail systems.

But this will work succussfully only if the following criteria are met:

1. You have well-defined specifications.
2. The project is subdivided so that each developer has unique responsibilities.
3. You have a strong management team that can keep all of the loose ends together.
4. Your team consists of mature, experienced software developers (typically who have worked together on previous projects) who can work with little to no supervision.
5. Team members require no training in software development skills or in the project's functionality.
6. You have a history of delivering products on schedule.

You might disagree with the above criteria, but if developers are not available for face-to face-communication, your leadership role will be much more difficult to enforce. In addition, your probability for success will be very low.

On the other hand, what do you do when individual developers wish to work at home?

If you allow selected developers to work at home, how do you justify this to other teams or team members who cannot work at home (or aren't allowed to work at home)? Unless you have total agreement among your managers, there is no way you should even attempt this.

In addition, if other groups do not perceive your organization as being successful, allowing developers to work at home is not going to help you (and development) win friends. In fact, development will be viewed as a prima donna organization that always seems to get its way: no dress code, flexible hours, and now—they can work at home!

I wouldn't recommend it!

What about contractors—do you allow them to work off-site?

Rules for the Unruly

Rule 82: If you must use contractors, make sure it is just for components.

There is one big exception: when the project can be handed to a contracting company that has extensive experience building all components of the product. I can think of several products that were completely and successfully "outsourced" to a contracting company.

Just make sure that you have arranged a deal that is a win-win for both parties. For the members of the party doing the work, you want them to commit to a project and schedule that is achievable and that can bring them reasonable money to grow their business. You certainly don't want them to go out of business. (You might need them on future projects!)

On the other hand, make sure that you have a contract that gives you access to all source code and documents, and includes non-compete clauses and the ability for you to reap the rewards in the marketplace. In other words, you'll want your company to receive the royalty stream (or whatever residual technique you all agree on) so that your organization will have the financial freedom to compete with other players that may have developed their products internally. You don't want to be burdened financially by the need to make huge royalty payments to a contractor.

Reality Checks

Check 44: Contractors that are completely responsible for an entire project usually fail.

Once, I set up a project (because of its low priority) consisting solely of contractors—except for a project manager who worked in our office. A *junior* project manager.

Well, the project was months late, the contractors cost us an "arm and a leg," and the end result was not that good. To add insult to injury, the contractor's knowledge left our company when the contractors finished the contract. Although you can't always do this, you need to place some performance criteria on the contractors.

For example, if you expect to build a custom database extractor that executes 20 times faster than the nearest competition, you had better build that expectation into the contract.

I learned my lesson: Only staff and organize projects that are set up to win. If you don't, the results that I had will most likely be yours as well.

Here's another lesson I've learned from taking over projects that had been populated solely by contractors: Time and time again, projects developed by consultants may sort of "hit the mark." But when you try to update them, you'll probably encounter a totally unmaintainable and definitely unstructured product. There is a difference between building products that work and building products that work *and* are properly designed to be enhanced. The development costs associated with restructuring undocumented source code is probably as great as the cost of starting over and doing it right.

Check 45: You get what you pay for with most overseas development contracts.

"Forget you guys! Let's just have the project done in India!" Ever heard that? Well, I sure have. When there is little confidence that your development shop can deliver, a common threat is to use contracting shops outside the U.S. (or whatever country your company calls home).

The software talent in other countries is outstanding. Nothing wrong with that. The use of contractors that cost one-third of the cost for a typical developer at home may be an attractive way to control the high cost of development.

On the other hand, take it from me: I've worked with consultants in countries where the labor costs are dramatically low, and it's still a money pit. I insisted that we have development management in both locations (both here in the United States and in the foreign country). I thought I had taken care of every risk.

Two results occurred:

1. The hidden cost of development was larger than I had expected. By hidden costs, I mean tools training, product training, and culture training. The need for overcommunicating basic issues was overwhelming. Accessibility became the foremost issue, since we started work when the foreign contractors ended their day.

2. The morale impact on our own developers took us to an all-time low. They viewed themselves as expendable and that it was only a question of time before they would be replaced by "outsiders."

Needless to say, after many months on one of these projects, I inevitably end up canceling the contract and bringing all of the work in-house for proper completion.

What a lesson to learn!

I have been pleasantly pleased with a software house in England that worked on analytical components of our software. They weren't responsible for the user interface, specifications were well laid out, and other major project components and milestones were handled at home. In fact, when we approached critical milestones, we automatically hauled them to our site. This approach can work well if properly managed and if the project is jointly owned. In this case, there was no threat to our own software engineers.

We would periodically send our folks "over there" and send their folks here. We made extensive use of electronic mail systems and there were planned periods where we would all work "under one roof." We didn't just contract out the whole project—only specific pieces that this foreign contractor had experience building. Our engineers could then concentrate on the parts that they did best.

Practical Maniac Tips

Tip 33: Get your managers together and initially, without marketing, review all of your projects currently being staffed.

For with this review, pretend that there are at least two other methods of delivering those products (through the use of contractors, for example).

Categorize these alternative approaches based on how they will impact schedules, headcount, and cost. Naturally, you will need to specify the positives and negatives for each approach.

Here's an example:

Project T
Option: Subcontract the graphics presentation engine
Schedule: Push forward the release date by one month
Headcount: Temporary addition of two contractors
Cost: Cost to project is approximately $55,000

Because this is a partnership, have your marketing managers join you and your managers in order to review the options. Nothing may change as a result of this workshop, but I guarantee that you will continue to reinforce your interest in finding the best, most efficient way to deliver products to market.

In Summary

Offices work, cubicles don't.

Forget the trends and provide a working environment that maximizes privacy and allows for uninterrupted time to accomplish goals. Cubicles do not inspire an atmosphere of open communication; leadership does.

Think of creative ways to improve any office arrangement.

There are all sorts of inventive ways to improve on productivity.

If you *do* allow developers to work at home . . . .

Be aware that some people will abuse the privilege and other organizations will view this as yet another "development benefit" that they don't enjoy.

Listening to Marketing

Is marketing development's friend, competitor, or enemy? The relationship between marketing and development is generally a very sensitive one for most software companies. Have you ever developed a project that failed in the market? If this happens, who's to blame?

This chapter explains the importance of staying close to customers, listening to marketing, and how to incorporate market strategy within day-to-day development life. I'll cover these topics:

- Importance of staying close to customers
- Cooperating and listening to marketing
- What if marketing wishes to "negotiate" directly with your developers?
- Negotiating product features
- Importance of customer support

Importance of Staying Close to Customers

Working closely with customers is normally regarded as a marketing and sales function. It makes sense for customer relations to be owned by those best suited to deal with customer needs. Developers usually don't excel at knowing how to deal directly with customers. On the road, I've attended many meetings where developers have been asked to present to customers. I'm often dumbfounded by the inability of developers to communicate product expectations appropriately.

Then again, is it the developer's fault?

At headquarters, it has not been unusual for a developer to approach a problem without much regard for specific customer requests. But in a direct confrontation with an "upset" customer, the same software engineer would backpeddle. Suddenly, the engineer would own the customer's problem and actually "sign up" with a schedule commitment! Unbelievable.

Rules for the Unruly

Rule 83: Prepare for customer meetings.

When a customer visit takes place, being unprepared can have worse consequences than not showing up at all. At a minimum, address the following issues *before* you meet with your customers:

1. Have your presentation rehearsed and timed. The last thing a customer wants is to spend three hours in a meeting that should have lasted for one hour.

2. Make sure that you understand your goals for the visit and relate them to the customer. At the end of the meeting, review the results and tie this review back to the original goal. This is vitally important.

3. Have a set of questions and answers ready. Chances are the customer will have some tough questions. *All* of your company's representatives need to have consistent answers for *all* customers they visit.

4. Let the customer know how confidential your presentation is—you don't need a premature "press leak."

5. Give customers a reward for their help. Some sort of plaque or free software would be appropriate and you'll find that customers don't forget these seemingly small gestures. A tee shirt that simply advertises your company is not what I have in mind!

Rule 84: Make customer visits mandatory.

Promising that customer needs come first is easy (in a speech), but actually delivering on that promise requires commitment. Getting the word out that your developers make routine "pilgrimages" to listen to customers is an incredible motivator to customers, executive management, the press, and especially to stockholders. Be sure to provide customers with examples of decisions you have made based on customer needs. The fact that you are genuinely responsive will spread from customer to customer like wild fire.

Rule 85: Usability tests have many benefits.

I know how difficult it is to plan the logistics involved in usability testing. But once you get started, you'll find that the benefits of conducting usability tests far outweigh any negatives. Here are some major benefits that I've witnessed:

1. Usability testing improves customer relations.

2. You get critical feedback on the user-friendliness of your product. If this is not critical to your products, you ought to

be building products for mainframes. (And you shouldn't be reading this book!)

3. The test results improve your relationship with your sales-people, who are typically not aware of the development efforts taking place at headquarters.

4. Usability test results, when they are taken seriously by development, can lead to improvements that considerably reduce future customer support calls.

5. The tests can motivate your developers, who tend to have limited exposure to customers.

6. Usability tests allow (or even force) marketing to take an active role in development by making sure that the bond between product and customer is being correctly implemented or designed.

Use this list with your sales and marketing counterparts to explain the need for usability tests. To this day, I still have to explain the benefits in detail to some marketing folks—others (the more brilliant types) "lock onto" the idea right away!

Reality Checks

Check 46: Is there time for usability testing?

How do you determine whether a project has been designed correctly? Since today's marketplace requires you to get new products to market faster (and faster and faster), is there really time to make sure some level of usability is achieved at the beginning of a project?

Believe it or not, I have seen situations where marketing has not wanted to expend the effort to perform any usability tests. Since there is always too little time and marketing already has a good understanding of what customers really want in a product's design, why bother? "Besides, it would cost money."

Without up-front user interface testing, you risk the success of your project. Some companies (namely, Microsoft and Lotus) spend a tremendous amount of money and time to validate user interfaces before committing to programming. Even if you are forced to minimize this activity, you should still get significant benefit.

To prove this statement, I'll offer a situation from personal experience. We rushed together a user interface plan, arranged for time in a user interface lab (one with a one-way mirror, tape equipment, personal computer, and so on), and brought in a few key customers to meet with our salesperson. The feedback was monitored by key members of the team. Even though testing was rushed and wasn't extensive, it was still a great learning experience for the development team.

And this particular usability test had another benefit. The customers "bought into" the project as partners. They appreciated being a part of the development process and became, as far as I was concerned, customers for life.

Check 47: Everyone should have customer contact.

Because I make it a firm commitment to expose everyone in development to customers, my managers typically arrange for every developer to have a "values session" with customers *at least* once per year. These sessions can take place during:

- User interface testing
- Trade shows
- A key milestone (such as beta), where a preliminary product will be presented to customers
- On-site "good will" visits

It is important to rehearse and plan for the visit beforehand. Usually, marketing should take the lead to make sure that the presentation is crisp and that the correct expectations will be set by all presenters.

At first, I admit, these customer sessions were not taken seriously by developers, but I quickly found that our sales organization looked forward to them because they could meet some of the "nerd herd," plus, it was great for their own client relations since the developer was frequently treated as a special guest.

Our competition didn't make the extra effort to get the nerd herd out, so our salespeople began treating these visits as "icing on the cake" in terms of closing sales. Sometimes, these visits would actually raise a customer's confidence in our quest to be customer oriented—which, of course, resulted in *more* business with that customer.

Rather than send our folks out in a totally arbitrary way, I have found that these events provide the best opportunity to get customers together with developers:

- **Beta visits with the beta software.** For customers, nothing is more thrilling than being handed a beta copy of software by one of the developers of that software. Also, with the developer on site, he or she can help install the software and can actually demonstrate key enhancements and benefits in a one-on-one setting.

- **Annual conference events.** If your company has an annual conference or road show, this is the perfect time to get your developers together with the "decision makers." As long as the dialog is carefully rehearsed and facilitated with marketing, the communication is beneficial not only for the customer but also for the developer.

- **Delivering documentation surveys.** On more than one occasion, our documentation people have hand-delivered documentation surveys to customers in order to receive feedback. On another occasion, customer support held a fun game for customers—including great prizes—in order to reinforce our customer-support activities. The point is that opportunities for pairing developers with customers are plentiful. And every development organization can participate!

 ## Practical Maniac Tips

Tip 34: Organize a usability field trip.

Pick one of your least risky products (small team, minimal enhancements) and, at the beginning of the project, set up a customer usability test. Choose a few customers (not more than three or four) and get their feedback on:

- Ease of use
- Flow—does the organization of the product and the way that the user maneuvers through the product make sense?
- Features—are they enough to warrant the release?
- Documentation and on-line early review of style and format

• Suggestions (from the customer)

To avoid taking a lot of time, allocate only two days for the development team to prepare and allocate a single day for the usability tests at your office. The sophisticated usability labs can wait. Make the test very simple to implement!

Tip 35: Place some personal attention on your next beta milestone.

At your next beta milestone, make it a point to have developers hand-deliver the beta software at customer on-site installations. If there is an expense issue and there are beta customers in your local area, then use them as local beta sites.

Cooperating and Listening to Marketing

Marketing is your partner, not development's enemy. The only enemy you have is the competition.

I can't tell you how many times I've heard developers talking in the halls about how "Marketing just doesn't understand;" "They want software delivered faster even if there are bugs in it;" and "Why aren't the products we've already delivered making money?" You've probably heard these or similar complaints.

There can be no blame here. Each organization (marketing, development, sales, and so on) has to own their particular accountabilities, and there must be trust that other organizations are fully capable of doing their respective jobs.

It sounds trite, but it's true: Trust is the cornerstone for building a team-driven working relationship. When marketing folks distrust development, they will always assume that development is not responding to the needs of the business.

When development folks distrust marketing, it may *still* look like development doesn't have its act together because development tends not to be well connected to the sales, finance, and executive organizations.

This whole marketing/development relationship can be a big problem, regardless of who is at fault—if there is a problem, chances are the whole company will be negatively affected.

Rules for the Unruly

Rule 86: Stop negative teamwork immediately.

As soon as you identify a problem that will affect teamwork, remove the problem. The longer you wait to confront the issue, the bigger the problem will become.

And you *will* eventually have to solve it.

Rule 87: Listen to marketing.

Make sure that, when product and strategic decisions are needed, the leadership is coming from marketing. Just as marketing may challenge your headcounts, implementation, and schedules, you also have the right to challenge marketing to justify revenue, competitive impacts, and other sales-related issues. But don't make the mistake, like many of my managers did, to publicly fight with marketing's strategic vision or direction.

Rule 88: Avoid feature creep.

If you want to intentionally derail the success of any software project, just allow "feature creep." This situation occurs when, even after a project is well underway, an overzealous marketing manager continues to ask for (and gets) enhancements.

If you don't care about delivering your product on schedule, allow feature creep. If you do care about delivering products to market on schedule, feature changes that were not originally considered *may* cause your project to spin out of control. And the awful thing here is that no one will own the schedule slip. Development will think that it is "being more flexible" and marketing will consider that "development just doesn't pull its weight." Executive management and sales will only remember one thing:

Development didn't deliver!

Train your development managers to recognize feature creep and, like a weed, spray it immediately! If you can accommodate a requested feature, document the change in team minutes and then build it into the product. There's a fine line here: You should avoid feature creep, but don't be inflexible. Sometimes an unplanned enhancement can be accommodated in the schedule and will make the difference between product acceptance or rejection!

On the other hand, *constant* request changes will eventually drain the life from your development teams. And, if you succumb to feature creep, you'll open an even bigger drain: When numerous changes must be absorbed in a project, a monster schedule slippage can result. The changes absorbed along the way will not only take up any and all possible schedule slack, but they will actually add to the schedule! This is when your development manager informs you that, "I don't know how it happened, but we're now three months behind schedule."

When too many features are requested *during* a product development cycle, this usually implies that marketing didn't do its homework at the *beginning* of the project. As a rule: The more junior the product manager, the more requests you'll receive for features throughout the project.

Rule 89: Without proper marketing, your product will eventually fail.

It is never enough just to have the correct number of product features. Without proper marketing, how can your company convince customers that they should purchase or upgrade to the product?

The following list is a starting point for marketing, and describes how even a little marketing can yield a lot in terms of sales. At minimum, marketing should provide for:

- proper positioning of the product against all competitive offerings. Marketing should clearly understand how the product will match customer needs and how well existing products meet those needs.

- a communication plan designed to show how the product fits into the company's "grand strategy."

- "seeding the press" so that benefits of the product are widely communicated at the time of (or just prior to) the release.

- getting the company "hyped up" for the forthcoming product release.

All of this is typically called the *product launch*. Development should have an appreciation of this important activity.

Rule 90: Don't negotiate "features wars;" instead, focus revisions.

Rather than spend months negotiating all of a product's features with marketing, agree on a base set of features as quickly as possible. When you spend too much time negotiating and justifying the elimination of certain features based on internal constraints, you waste valuable time that could have been spent actually implementing critical features.

Before you begin product development, marketing should already have thoroughly resolved feature requirements based on these basic criteria:

* Customer need
* Competitive offerings
* Industry trends and expectations

If this research has been satisfactorily completed, basic product features can be decided in a matter of a few short weeks. Negotiation of features is the toughest (and usually an unplanned for) part of most project schedules. Yet the pain and schedule delays caused by mismanaging this negotiation tends to be repeatedly ignored by marketing and other senior management. Correct the problem at the outset of a project and I guarantee the rest of the project will go smoothly (provided that you manage developers well, of course).

 Reality Checks

Check 48: Watch public encounters.

During difficult times, "blame tossing'" is as prevalent as cow-chip tossin' in Texas. In one specific meeting where action items were passed around, marketing (in typical fashion) was the recipient of several items. These actions centered around:

* Reevaluating pricing (maybe there is a pricing problem)
* Use of value added resellers (VARs) as another distribution avenue
* Repackaging (and hence, renaming) of an older less functional product that could excite the low end market

Development received very few action items—in fact, only one. But we *could* have been the recipient of many action items, namely:

- Hire testers immediately to straighten out quality problems.
- Reduce functionality by some percentage in a yet-to-be-released product so that the product can ship this fiscal year.
- Redesign the user interface since customers are *not* buying due to ease-of-use problems.

Because we believed that we had our act together, we felt little need to adjust our current resources. Unfortunately, marketing made a bold statement:

"Marketing never gets off the hook! Why don't you give development half of the action items we get? Let's get products out dramatically faster—we all know that development `sandbags' its schedules."

The room was silent. My own managers were looking at me, wondering what to say or do. I wasn't sure myself—so, rather than charge and ruin our development credibility, I sat back and smiled nervously. I think everyone in the room knew that I was very agitated by this remark, but that I wouldn't stoop to a similar retort for the sake of saving face.

My managers were so infuriated with the derogatory statements made by marketing that they demanded to have a "skip level" meeting with the president. Their intent was to silence the obviously distrustful V.P. of marketing.

So why did the developers insist on elevating the issue? Development managers rightfully had a certain amount of pride in their work and, as far as they were concerned, there was a good reason that development had only a single action item.

They knew how to deliver software products to market and had established an outstanding track record in doing just that—delivering. There was *no* sandbagging. Development made incredible efforts to deliver on marketing's expected and (sometimes) unrealistic delivery schedule. In fact, we all thought we were part of a great team.

The president actually set up a forum to address the complaints and, although a very stressful set of meetings followed, the development managers eventually were vindicated. That took guts—taking a senior V.P. to task!

But the development managers knew they were justified. This represents another example of "doing the right thing."

What would have happened if they hadn't spoken up?

The results are not too difficult to imagine.

If the disparaging comments were allowed and accepted, they would have spread rapidly throughout the company. The message would have been that a serious development issue existed. Others in lesser marketing roles would have continued to expand on the negative comments and this "disease" would have spread throughout other nondevelopment organizations.

A worst case is when the developers in your organization overhear these comments. You then have a serious morale problem. And from that point forward, your developers would probably lack confidence in marketing and in their own managers. In this scenario, development managers were able to control the problem before it exploded down to the level of individual developers.

Check 49: Decisions need to be made that benefit the customer and your bottom line.

Our development organization actually made product decisions based on marketing direction, which, for a technology-driven company, was a groundbreaking approach. Other software companies made product decisions based on where they felt the technology was advancing. But our teams made decisions based on what was right for the customer.

I can think back to product decision meetings where I would not make a decision unless we got the proper feedback from marketing. But in this company, marketing had less stature than development, and I couldn't understand that.

In fact, in high-level meetings, I had to explain to executive management why development should consult with marketing about product decisions. For instance, I stressed the need for answers to these basic questions:

1. If we do this project, will there be any negative revenue impact?

2. Since we have U.S. salespeople in the room, let's make sure that we get international feedback before we commit.

3. How will our competition respond?

Nobody else in the room was qualified to answer these questions—only marketing! Of course, everyone had opinions, but nobody in development, support, sales, or operations could be held accountable for their responses. Only marketing had ownership of the issues that I raised. Marketing folks, like any members of a team, appreciate being part of a solution. I always make sure that I "work the team members" as equally as possible (more on this later in the chapter).

Check 50: There must be a better way to negotiate features with marketing.

Although I've made reference to this topic in other parts of the book, I should stress here that features negotiation with marketing is one of the most critical parts of the development process, and one that continues to plague the effectiveness of software projects.

I couldn't understand the constant implications made by marketing that development wasn't delivering projects on schedule, because we continually hit the major design and implementation schedule milestones. So, my development managers investigated. We found that schedules for new products and even product revisions were being consumed by four to six months of negotiations on feature sets with marketing.

What?

This problem didn't just exist for *new* projects—but for *any* project!

Figures 7.1–7.3 show some of the methods typically used to determine which features are included in a project revision, for example, a product upgrade.

Figure 7.1 shows what I would call the "feature exhaustion" technique.

Here is how it goes:

1. Marketing decides that a new project needs to be initiated.
2. Marketing reviews the feature and bug database to see what needs to be put into the next product release.
3. Marketing writes a list of enhancements that must be in the next revision and presents it to development.
4. Development management asks for the features to be prioritized.

Figure 7.1 Feature exhaustion method of deciding feature sets

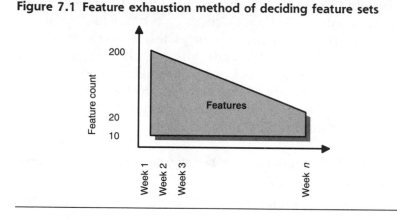

5. Marketing says, "How can I make decisions when I don't know how much time it takes to create each feature?"

6. Development answers, "It's not that easy to just put man-hour or man-day estimates on projects. *Please* help us concentrate on those features that you need."

The exchange between steps 5 and 6 can continue almost indefinitely. Now look at the results:

- **Marketing.** Upset ("ticked off" is more like it) that they had to give up so many feature enhancements.

- **Development.** Exhausted and feeling a little "run through the wringer" since the weeks of negotiation could have taken far less time if only marketing had been reasonable to begin with.

By the way, I assume that feature requests are not determined by:

1. Funding dollars (I'll give your development organization $50,000 for feature X; otherwise, you get no money)

2. Number of customer requests (although this can be an important factor)

3. Product "hunches" with no direct validation from customers

The next technique, shown in Figure 7.2, is one I call "Money talks."

Figure 7.2 "Money talks" feature negotiation technique

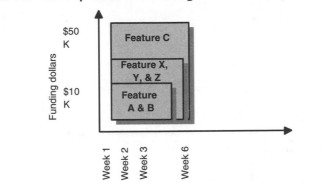

Under this technique, features are "voted" based on funding dollars, which are determined by marketing or sales organizations. In other words, the features that are to be included in the project must be estimated by development and then covered by specific funds, as determined by marketing (or sales).

When the funds "dry up," the features that have already been paid for become the features placed in the product. It's that simple.

And that ridiculous.

The technique shown in Figure 7.2 can use less time to decide feature sets than the technique portrayed in Figure 7.1. Look at the results of this approach, as they relate to funding (by organization):

- **Marketing.** Wishes they had more money to vote for features that didn't find their way into the product. They can't exactly explain this technique to customers without the customers becoming upset.

- **Development.** Forced to monitor each feature's expenses (a true management drain) while constantly juggling people to justify matching work with feature expense budget.

This approach is guaranteed to fail.

The last technique, shown in Figure 7.3, is my favorite: the "product theme."

Under this approach, marketing determines the project's overriding "theme" and then focuses most features that solve

Figure 7.3 Feature negotiation based on product theme

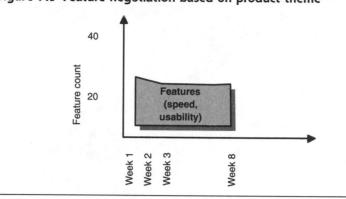

this theme. The number of features never changes much during the feature negotiation period.

In fact, there really is never much negotiation, even though other features (outside of the defined scope) can still be addressed. The length of time required here may be longer than the "voting for dollars" technique, but it sure is less painful. Here are the results (again, by organization):

- **Marketing.** A feeling of teamsmanship and "doing the right thing" prevails—the team works hard at solving a few key problems rather than wrestling through a seemingly endless barrage of meetings.

- **Development.** Feature negotiations are more of a creative process by focusing the developers on a project's scope rather than constantly re-addressing timing estimates. As a result, the project will probably be more successful, since fewer software modules in the product will be touched by what is typically a "let's add features everywhere" syndrome.

This product theme approach is the preferred technique, although I rarely see projects developed this way. Companies that focus on a few key elements tend to have better luck releasing projects on schedule.

Although this is covered in more detail in the next chapter, I would like to briefly mention projects that are developed using object-oriented technology (like C++). Projects that use object-oriented technology may initially take longer to build than projects that use other programming approaches, but revisions can be completed dramatically faster because lower-level objects are less likely to require changes.

Practical Maniac Tips

Tip 36: *Get some outside facilitation if your relationship with marketing needs improvement.*

One of the best learning opportunities involved a meeting hosted by a marketing strategist. His job was to facilitate product and strategic building efforts between the development and marketing leadership. I'll describe his approach.

The session should, at most, take one week of a consultant's time and should leave all participants with a better understanding of how development and marketing management should co-exist. Periodically, workshops like this can help energize your working relationships. It's a good idea to plan for this type of exchange once a year.

One warning: Most consultants will attempt to wrangle a long-term contract with you. Don't fall victim to it. Use consultants sparingly.

Bypassing Development Management

You should produce a work environment (culture) that is open and free enough to stimulate creative communication and brainstorming. How do you handle a situation where your developers feel more comfortable working directly with marketing than with their own development managers? Or vice versa where marketing wants to deal directly with developers, bypassing development managers?

Rules for the Unruly

Rule 91: *Define your role as a development manager.*

Your development managers should provide leadership yielding the following benefits:

1. Career coaching and performance evaluation of team members.

2. Ability to detect major risks and to help the team remove major issues that are out of the team's control.

3. Team leadership that improves team performance based on past experience.

4. Assistance to make sure that the team stays focused and team dependencies are managed.

5. Collection of technical information and evaluation of software tools that will help save valuable development time. (I really believe in this, since it will help reinforce a manager's technical ability.)

In my humble opinion, "killer" development managers *are* the difference between an outstanding versus mediocre organization.

If marketing believes that your managers have any of the following negative roles, you either have a severe development leadership problem or product marketing just doesn't understand the role of development:

1. Development management "snuffs out" creativity.

2. The product manager could easily manage the developers better.

3. Developers believe they can deliver products faster without the constant management attention.

4. Developers believe they should be empowered to "run their own show."

Solve these problems fast. If you don't, your development organization could essentially "self-destruct."

Reality Checks

Check 51: Let's form a separate company.

I've been confronted with the following situation at least twice. Pretend you provide development with the following basic ingredients:

1. Tablespoon of leadership

2. Quart of teammanship

3. Twists of decision criteria based on company, customer, then employee priority

4. And, of course, a history of cooking the final product right, every time

When you follow this recipe, what do you have? A development organization that's "second to none" and a marketing organization that sometimes thinks the spirit of "spontaneity and creativity" is forever gone!

I bet most of you have found yourself in this kettle.

To make this long story short, overzealous product marketing manager, feel that it would better serve the company to take the team outside of the normal structure.

In one case, a product manager actually wrote memos explaining how the team should be completely under his control, "outside of the watchful eyes" of development management. He even went so far as to search for office space away from our facility. Senior management did nothing—if it could get products out sooner, why not let the product manager have his way?

Well, I quickly battled back with hard-charging memos directed at the product manager and the executive management team. Within about two weeks, I was able to regroup development under my control. The memos I sent were actually reaffirmations of the teamsmanship that meant so much within development. And my memos were reviewed by all of my development managers *before* they were released.

In a second case, a product manager actually received executive approval to take a planned project and manage it himself, even though he had no experience leading development. In fact, the arrangement was close to being set up as a separate consulting company. Because I think I am always receptive to better ways to deliver products, the discussion I had concerning this "opportunity" with the senior executives was interesting and also frustrating. Both groups tried to convince me to give up this team, but all of their arguments were illogical to me.

In their view, letting the product manager deliver the project with outside sources would:

• Be cheaper to the company.
• Deliver the product to market much sooner.

As we talked, the discussions became even more interesting:

• The product manager wanted to quit the company and contract back to us.

- The development team would be the same team that was originally scheduled for the project.

- There had been no discussion with my development manager regarding issues that might have justified this radical departure.

What problem was really being solved? It became pretty clear—the product manager wanted the opportunity to create his own company at the company's expense. This whole episode took lots of time to resolve. The situation could have been avoided if senior product management had understood what the product manager really was up to.

The moral of these stories?

If your teams are outside of your control and if your company encourages lots of third-party development activities, you will be left with a product strategy and implementation results that are as chaotic to your customers as they are to your development staff.

Check 52: We don't need no stinkin' management!

I was delivering a poor performance review (actually, the *review* was good, but the engineer had been delivering poor performance) when, to my surprise, the employee stated, "My performance would have been a lot better if our team members managed themselves." He went on: "In fact, new management books indicate that modern development requires self-managed teams."

I cleared my throat.

There was silence for about ten seconds.

I began, "First, I appreciate the fact that you are reading management books and periodicals. I'm sure that there are software organizations that practice self-management. One of the reasons we are having this discussion is that your manager recognized that your performance is impacting your team's performance. The team is empowered to deliver on project component goals. However, I empower the development manager to be responsible for the overall team performance. As long as I'm in charge, I will never expect a team to self-rule, since I believe someone needs to take overall responsibility and accountability for the team."

Need I say more?

Practical Maniac Tips

Tip 37: Reinforce the role of development management with your teams.

With your development managers, enumerate all of the benefits that they provide to your development teams. Then, verify these same benefits with your development teams. I guarantee that you will hear negative feedback from the teams. List these negatives as well and then do something about them. Here are some negatives that you might hear from your developers:

- Managers schedule too many meetings
- Managers are not in touch with the team's issues

Tip 38: Reaffirm your development manager's roles outside of development.

Once you get complete agreement of your own management role within development, set up a team building meeting with marketing and communicate it. If there is marketing disagreement, then solve the difference of opinion. Don't wait for a crisis to take place in order to clear the air.

Did We Forget Customer Support?

Your customer support technicians can tell you:

- What "works" and what "doesn't work" in your products.
- Feature improvements that would reduce customer frustration.
- New features that customers are requesting most frequently.

Is this information important to you? I bet it is—and also to marketing.

Rules for the Unruly

Rule 92: Customer support should be part of development.

Customer support is traditionally part of marketing or operations. I think the reason stems from the word "customer" in customer support.

But why not move customer support into development?

One "opportunity" that I've wanted to provide is for the documentation organization to be "evaluated" based on the effectiveness of customer support. Another "opportunity" is to get feedback from customer support regarding bugs and feature requests.

For these two reasons, I've never regretted having development and customer support under one roof. If you do integrate the organizations, make sure that you call your group something like "Development and Support." Give customer support due credit.

 Reality Checks

Check 53: Track support problems from "cradle to grave."

You definitely need an automated way to track customer calls so that you can respond constructively to repetitive complaints. There ought to be a way, however, to link specific customer problems to your internal bug-tracking database. I'll explain more about this in Chapter 8. Also put a fax board on a network so your support people can fax responses automatically to customers.

Check 54: How important is customer support to development?

Our most recent annual employee survey showed that one of development's main requests was to integrate customer support into the mainstream product development process. Customer support rarely heard what was happening "over there" (in development).

As a response, we held monthly meetings with customer support and development management to review the key issues that customer support was hearing from customers. As a later action, we integrated customer support within the development organization.

As we "folded" customer support under development, *problem categories* began to be tracked based on customer problem calls.

I was determined to help customer support become a valuable influence on the development process. Once we started categorizing customer calls, we were able to recognize that our product's installation process needed some attention.

Figure 7.4 Call volume before proper attention

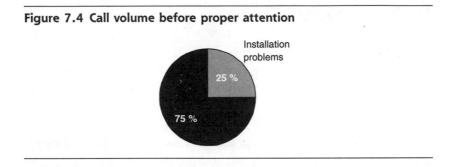

Approximately 25 percent of our call volume was based on customers installing our software, as shown in Figure 7.4.

We improved both the installation program and the associated documentation. Our call volume associated with product installation practically disappeared, as shown in Figure 7.5.

Unbelievable.

Practical Maniac Tips

Tip 39: Force the product teams to accept customer support into the fold.

Set up a meeting where you can ask the development and customer support management teams to determine how to work together more closely. At a minimum, invite customer support to participate in your regular development meetings. Over time, it will make sense to all concerned to fold support into your organization.

Figure 7.5 Call volume after proper attention

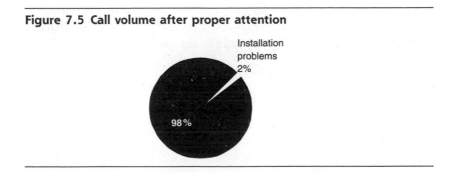

In Summary

Stay close to your customers.

Although this is typically a marketing job, your development organization needs to be closely aligned with your customer base.

Cooperate, listen, and take product direction from marketing.

Make sure that your bond with product marketing is consistent with everyone's major goal: producing the best products for your customer base.

Keep control of your development teams.

If you arbitrarily let teams out of your "management sight," your development infrastructure will gradually disintegrate. Would marketing let another organization supply product managers? Would your sales V.P. want development to have its own sales force? Of course not! If there is a problem, solve it within development—you don't need to form other software organizations to solve an internal problem.

Make sure your development management is effective.

Just because you have good managers doesn't mean that their teams are effective. You, as the development leader, need to constantly check that your managers are getting the most from their teams.

Don't ignore customer support.

You have a gold mine of information under your nose in customer support. They can help dramatically improve customer satisfaction—if you bring them into the picture.

Guiding Your Technology Future

Rather than providing more reality checks in this final chapter, I want to present issues that affect the way developers build industry-standard products. At the current pace of technology innovation, it is almost impossible to settle into one set of tools: every six months, state-of-the-art tools will have become state-of-the-past. If your developers stick with one internal technology and do not keep up with these industry innovations, your company might have the opportunity to learn about "Chapter 11 technology" (bankruptcy protection). But if your developers are continually jumping from one technology base to another, confusion can be the long-term result, and customers would definitely become confused. So what do you do?

In this final chapter, I'll cover:

- Key industry history and trends that can affect the way you run your organization
- How to develop a technology vision
- Techniques on getting to market faster
- Keeping the customer happy with your products, upgrades, and services
- Keeping each of your organizations current with state-of-the-art technology

The Industry: 1970s and 1980s

The software business, in its heyday, looked like an endless growth industry. Venture capitalists were pouring millions into an industry that returned high yields in the 1970s and early 1980s. In what other industry can you change a suggested retail price (SRP) of $200 and up for a product whose cost of goods sold (COGs) is in the $15 range? In many of my visits to the best software companies, business controls seemed conspicuously absent. Controls? Who needs 'em? Customers were everywhere, funding was plentiful, and business was booming—nothing could go wrong. In retrospect, it somewhat reminds me of the Texas oil boom several years back.

What has been the price of entry into the software market? A good idea, a personal computer, and a talent to deliver on that idea. Garage shops cropped up everywhere, and often produced outstanding products. Visicalc, Microsoft, Digital Research, Living VideoText, The Software Garden, Software Publishing, IUS, Peter Norton, and Ashton-Tate are some of the home-grown businesses. How many of these high-flyers are still left?

Some perceived the folks creating these products to be innovators or hackers. No rules—just invent and sell a technology that emulates creative ideas, then stand back and watch the cash flow! Some of the early marketing promotions and plans were rather humorous but seemed to appeal to purchasers, whose thirst for new creative applications bordered on addiction.

The Industry: 1990s and Beyond

Many of these early garage shops have long since gone out of business or have been gobbled up by larger companies. Of the thousands of startups that were in vogue just ten years ago, only a handful have continued to grow and prosper: Microsoft, Lotus, WordPerfect, Aldus, Computer Associates, and Borland come to mind. The competition has become too intense to allow poorly managed software shops to survive.

As the surviving companies become the IBMs of the 1990s, the direction of the industry remains steady: Software and software servicing (or customization) is where the growth is.

But what about hardware companies? Funding for hardware ventures is becoming increasingly difficult. The potential exists for high growth (in unit volume), but hardware companies must be aware that:

- Competition is fierce and profit margins in the 3- to 5-percent gross profit range are typical (usually based on expectations of high unit volume shipments).
- When technology changes, unsold products and inventory immediately becomes obsolete. (This is very costly dealing with hardware.)
- Excellent customer support and rapid delivery (to customers) were once a hardware company's sales weapons, but with the proliferation of PCs being sold to novices, the demands for ease-of-use and instantaneous assistance are becoming requirements.
- Global labor costs in building hardware components help determine which companies can survive especially in the United States.

To summarize, hardware products must have competitive features and outstanding support while being priced as a commodity (just like stereo equipment, televisions, and VCRs). Is it any surprise that more and more hardware companies see a better future in software? That's exactly what happened with Next and Novell.

What about the future of software?

- Competition is fierce and the remaining market share (for the rest of us after Microsoft, Lotus, Borland, and WordPerfect take their greedy portions) is incredibly small.

- Price competition is forcing software to be priced as a commodity (falling closer and closer to the $99 range).
- Due to the presence of outstanding application building tools, almost anyone can put together solutions.
- Although we software developers may sometimes feel that all of the "good product ideas have been used up," I am constantly proven wrong (Shapeware's ViSiO, for example, has changed the way we think of drawing).
- As products become more "interchangeable" by conforming to graphical standards (i.e., Windows), customers are switching to better products when presented with competitive upgrade pricing. (This implies little brand loyalty.)

The competitive pressure to provide better features than those found in other products is causing software providers to concentrate on their added value while using "plug and play" components for everything else.

Who benefits from this competitive environment? The customer, for one. The choices in software products have never been better. Some industry watchers had said that the newer environments (i.e., Windows) would stifle creativity! The opposite has happened. In only a few years following the release of Windows 3.0, Windows applications have bypassed the unit volume of DOS applications *worldwide*! Graphics products are a lot easier to use—Apple proved that years ago!

Developing a Vision

In software development, it's not enough to have a successful process in place. At any time, you may find yourself "blindsided" by:

- A competitive threat you didn't expect
- Attrition of key developers
- A technology shift (for instance, laptop computing to PDAs)

You, as a leader, owe it to your company (and to development) to provide a "bought-in," meaningful, and strategic *vision* of technology. This strategic vision can then be used to create a roadmap that your organization can follow. Your vision also must communicate what you, as the leader, believe. Even if your company's business (or marketing) strategy is weak or nonexistent, make sure that development has a vision. And put this vision into words.

Here are some of the topics that should be included in a vision document:

- Views on teamwork
- Where your organization's added value is going to be focused on
- Priorities
- Technologies on which you are standardizing
- Common component design
- Re-affirmation of who the customer is and how you'll satisfy customer needs
- Statement of product architecture
- A clear understanding of the technology trends that are most important to you

Consider an example of a combined development strategy and mission statement:

> Development's mission is to provide state-of-the-art product technologies that focus on customer needs first. When it comes to satisfying customer needs, this implies the following:
>
> - Ease-of-use, where every product created will undergo intensive usability testing—it is our intent for every product to be learned in less than one hour
> - Our products are no longer based just on U.S. needs; our products are designed with the global customer in mind
>
> Our strategy will be based on our ability to provide comprehensive functionality, regardless of the user's platform of choice. In other words, we are the leading vendor that provides solutions that work consistently on OS/2, Windows, and Macintosh platforms. Because of this strength, we endorse the use of common technology to minimize any development redundancies. For that reason, we've chosen C++ as the best language to use in building products that are portable and extendible.
>
> Our quality assurance techniques will continue to exploit automatic testing tools and comprehensive bug-tracking systems that enable instant communication of issues as they occur in our product development process. Documentation is an equal partner in our development

activities, participating in usability testing, on-line help creation, and documentation writing. From this point on, all documentation will be easily accessible on CD ROM.

Rather than invent a technology, we will make every effort to absorb or partner with technologies that get us to market faster.

In summary, it is our aim to provide global products aimed at customer satisfaction—with better documentation, higher product quality, complete features, and ease-of-use.

The previous statement provides a vision that communicates technology leadership. Here's a checklist of requirements that you can use to make sure that your statement passes the "vision test":

❏ **Can you communicate a comprehensive vision in just a few sentences?** If you can't, anyone reading it will be bored. Most technology vision statements are so long and complicated that they do not communicate understanding or confidence to the reader. Make it simple.

❏ **Was the vision really bought in?** Any strategic vision should include input from your managers and key development personnel. Also, verify it with other organizations and key customers. By the way, don't forget to pass it by the personnel department (excuse me—I mean human resources) since excerpts from the vision could help in key hiring campaigns.

❏ **The vision should communicate to a wide audience.** Rewrite your technical vision if it does not communicate to both a technical and non-technical audience.

❏ **Make it well-rounded—don't just emphasize "engineering."** A technology vision may emphasize engineering direction. But if the quality assurance and technical publications groups report to you (and they should), these organizations will need strategic direction, too. In a customer's eyes, product quality and outstanding documentation aids may be equally as important as product functionality!

❏ **Pretend you are a developer in your organization.** If you were a developer in your organization, would this vision help you focus on what you are currently building and what you should be building in the future?

If you don't have a vision or yours does not pass the "vision test," you definitely need to correct this oversight.

Fast to Market

Have you been the target of comments like the ones below? "If development could release product faster, the way our competition does, we could really win!"

Marketing and sales are routinely frustrated by the amount of time it takes to release software. They see early prototypes and can't believe that it takes months to turn those "screen shots" into working product. I have an analogy why this is so: People who routinely construct rough drafts of memorandums on a word processor discover that is relatively easy to turn those drafts into finished documents. They expect software development to be just as easy, but the comparison doesn't work. The program logic, algorithms, bug tracking, integration with other components, and validation all take place behind the scenes—away from the eyes of marketing and salespeople. These tasks cannot be represented in a prototype, although they represent the bulk of time spent on developing a product. The screen design and layout are relatively easy to create.

Despite the conflicting view of development and marketing, I can offer some advice on getting product to market fast, in a way that should make marketing and sales less upset and that can actually rejuvenate your development teams.

Rules for the Unruly

Rule 93: Agree on goals, validate that you're building the right product, and get seriously involved.

During a project, have you ever wondered whether the product being developed will actually match what the product must do? "Are we really building the right product?" Marketing, sales, and development must be accessible to each other when questions like these need to be answered.

Some organizations even go to extremes by making sure cubicles for all members of a team are positioned next to each other. But proximity is not as important as accesibility. (By the way, if you haven't yet read my views on cubicles, please refer to Chapter 6.)

Rule 94: Make well-informed decisions quickly.

Development always seems to be rife with problems: Feature creep, decisions are taking too long, "I never get a crisp answer" and so on.

At the end of the day (British folks use this phrase frequently—I kinda like it), you will either be remembered for being late to market or for getting your product out on or ahead of schedule. With quality. The fact that you couldn't hire, or that marketing never nailed down the feature sets, or that you lost a key engineer—these problems are always forgotten. The team needs to own the project and all should take the responsibility to resolve issues on schedule. In the early part of a product development cycle (you know, the specification and design stages), countless days are often lost due to team and management indecision. The early part of the schedule deserves the *most* attention to make sure that well-informed decisions are made quickly.

Why even say "well-informed"? Managers have a tendency to make a decision based solely on their personal perceptions about the issue or problem. "If my initial decision proves wrong," you tell yourself, "I can always change it later." Not so with software development.

Imagine that a decision is made on a given feature's implementation as dictated by marketing and that, after the development team implements it, sales says that the implementation is incorrect. Who bears the responsibility? Although this situation could simply be the result of miscommunication, it's more likely that the proper verification (or buy in) did not take place.

But gathering information should not prevent you from making quick decisions. I hear continuously that "it takes too long to get everyone together to make a decision. In fact, too many people's opinions can make decision making impossible." Those statements couldn't be further from the truth.

Undoing a poorly researched decision is far worse than the additional time required to adequately research a decision. You, as a development or marketing leader, can truly prove your leadership ability by learning how to get to the proper decision quickly. And this involves the ability to communicate with your peers and other organizations within the company and to sift through conflicting opinions.

If you (or one of your managers) have great difficulty handling contradictory opinions or a fundamental inability to properly communicate, software team leadership will be very difficult. If you develop a reputation for "brute forcing" decisions, you might as well find another line of work. A development team needs the ability to be creative and to brainstorm alternatives, but they especially need to be coached and led in a manner that provides closure to a problem. As you might suspect, by no means am I talking about consensus leadership here; it's close to impossible to get 100-percent agreement on any decision.

Rule 95: Prevent "decision indecision."

How can development force major product issues to be closed? Easy. As a team, you need to agree on a decision-making time frame to commit to the delivery dates that marketing has requested. I have rarely heard marketing say, "Boy, those development guys are forcing me to make decisions in an unrealistic time frame!" For the good of the project, avoid "decision indecision" by making it clear that, if a decision is not made by a given date, you will default to a specific course of action. Document this in team minutes.

Think about how you might have used this technique on your own projects. You'll probably be able to picture the project proceeding more smoothly.

Rule 96: Prototype early and get sign-off.

A semi-working prototype can really help a team work through program flow issues before code is committed. It's even better if the prototype can be developed using a technology that can actually generate code. Two excellent examples in the Windows C++ world are Visual C++ and ProtoView's excellent Protogen+ prototyping code generators.

Have I neglected to mention what you should do with prototypes? Get written acceptance of the prototype from the team (especially marketing) and place this documentation in your project notebook. (You do keep a binder for each project, don't you?) You can also use the prototype when key customers visit to show them your product direction.

You can, of course, update the prototype during product development. However, if the prototype uses tools that do not match the tools used to build the product, it will probably not make sense to update the prototype in sync with development of the actual product. The maintenance of the prototype will have little benefit.

Rule 97: Manage mini-milestones to avoid the "big flop."

I've already described milestones in some detail (see Chapter 5). But how do you manage so that you reach those milestones on time? If you wait for the entire team to attain alpha status, chances are you are in for a real "letdown." Certain members of the development team are just not going to be able to gain some level of closure at the same time as other team members. And if a major milestone is missed, what does that say about the status of the project? Certain project sub-systems are also much more complex than others.

As an aside, when I was a programmer, I remember designing a simple program at the same time as another programmer who was given the same task. The manager watched us both. I wrote a simple spec, got my manager's approval, and wrote the code. Rather than just execute the code after it all compiled with no errors, I ran some tests on a couple of the module interfaces (I found some integration mistakes!), and used the debugger to step through the most critical parts. The other programmer didn't want to "waste time" writing anything down. He wrote the code and just executed it. Obviously, his program didn't work. His clever program accidentally "reached the directory structure on his fixed disk drive" and royally upset our manager. My project was done by the end of that day. The other programmer stayed until midnight building his project—and it still didn't work very well! True story.

Using the approach that the other programmer followed is often a time-saving preference of developers. If you lead projects using that approach, you are going to pay the consequences in false starts. And, contrary to popular belief, time to market is actually faster when you take mini-steps.

You can dramatically show progress by planning frequent software integration mini-steps. Your confidence in attaining alpha on time will improve and your quality assurance folks will be a lot happier than if you don't wait to perform a monster integration at, say, alpha. Without mini-milestone integrations, major integrations can be a tremendous team headache.

Here's an approach that I've found to be successful: Near the start of the project, make sure all user interfaces can be invoked and that all module sub-systems can be integrated. This implies that all major module application programming interfaces (APIs) are defined. If you have the luxury to do so (and I hope you do), these APIs can be exported to your quality assurance team members so that they can write test software that exercises these module interfaces. You'll be amazed at the integration problems you'll avoid by implementing this modular testing approach.

Solving integration problems early will substantially reduce risk—which in turn should result in schedules that are met! Nice.

Keeping the Customer Happy

Customer satisfaction extends far beyond the obvious need to provide technical support. You also need to keep key customers informed about new product features and release dates, and you need to provide updates under a schedule that is timely yet not too frequent. In addition, you need to actively cultivate new customers. All of this is much easier said than done.

Demonstration Software

Why even talk about demonstration software? Well, demonstration software provides an effective tool for closing potential business and can help current customers plan for future upgrades. I think it's important to discuss these components of demonstration software:

- Pricing
- Screen show or live?
- Support

Many software vendors charge a nominal fee (typically less than $10) for demonstration software. If a customer decides to purchase the software, this fee is usually subtracted from the purchase price. What do I think about this approach? Forget it. The paperwork and overhead required to process these "nominal fees" is not worth your time. It's also not worth the customer relations problems that can result when customers ask themselves: "Why is this company charging me to view what amounts to an advertisement for their product and is not really a full working product?"

Words of advice: *Give* away demonstration software.

Computerized slide shows of screen shots with some annotation can be an extremely effective way to walk a customer through a contrived demonstration path. Unfortunately, a brief demonstration slide show may lead to many more questions than you will be able to answer.

If your software has the capability of providing a completely functional working version (with some restrictions, of course), your customer can play with most of your software's features. Consider some feature restrictions that are most effective:

- No file saving
- No printing (or printing with a background on each page with something like the word "DEMO" on each page)
- Key features implemented with simplified functionality (for example, a communications program that only supports a 1200 baud rate)

Now consider some feature restrictions that *upset* customers:

- Embedded timers (where product fails to work after a certain number of hours)
- Key features are missing that may be required for normal operation
- Features that work only a specific number of times

A mini-manual (whether on paper or on-line) will aid in your potential customer's enjoyment.

How do you turn demonstration software into a real product? Some companies provide demonstration software that (through a password or a downloadable DLL module available from your company's bulletin board system) can magically convert a demonstration into a fully working application.

One notable company experimented with this approach in the late 1980s. They discovered that their so-called "easy-conversion" approach became a logistical support nightmare. (The company is no longer in business.) Don't waste your time. If a potential customer likes your demonstration software, they should be able to call you or a dealer to order a real package for immediate delivery.

Copy Protection and Site Licensing

You need to protect your investment. Copy protection is still extremely popular with niche (in other words, vertical) market application providers. But customers actually *hate* it. They understand your need to protect your product from illegal duplication. But they can't stand the fact why you, as a software provider, do not trust them. And, the license agreement they are supposed to follow? Have you read one lately?

They're usually impossible to comprehend.

Borland did the industry a service years ago by presenting a license agreement entitled "No-nonsense License." Not only was it simple to understand, it actually was realistic. No copy protection, and no restrictions other than: "Treat this software as you would a paperback book."

Two extraordinary software developers, Frame Technology and Micrografix, have taken licensing simplification a step further. They recognized that it is increasingly common for corporate customers to have a desktop at the office and a laptop at home (or for travel). But did you know that, with most software licensing agreements, it is illegal to have a software application installed on both systems? These two vendors allow their software to be used by one individual on up to two systems to accommodate the home-office (or frequent traveler) trend.

Unless your software has a high price tag exceeding $5,000, copy protection should be enforced by the user and not through inconvenient devices that need to be installed on a customer's system. Site licensing on a network can also be difficult to enforce because you, as the software provider, would like to get proper revenue from all users who have the right to use the software. Customers, on the other hand, may feel they should only pay for the number of licenses that will normally be used at one time (also known as "concurrent user licensing").

I have the following suggestions for resolving copy protection issues:

- Join the Software Publishers Association (SPA) to demonstrate your commitment to treating computer software as a licensed asset. If your software is illegally copied, the SPA can help you enforce major infractions. The SPA can be reached at:

  Software Publishers Association
  1101 Connecticut Ave., NW
  Suite 901
  Washington, DC 20036

  Don't forget to use the SPA warning notice in one of your opening screens during your application's installation process. It doesn't hurt to also prominently display the SPA warning in a help screen (or in your product's About dialog box).

- For site licensing purposes, I recommend third-party "concurrent user" metering software. Network administrators can use these readily available products to self-monitor concurrent use (or specific individual use) on a network. To build network licensing software into your product, you must enable recovery for user's personal computer crashes, provide network support, temporarily allow users to exceed the maximum limit, and so on.

- For individual licensing, provide a registration card with the serial number pre-printed (or already labeled). This serial number should be kept in your customer database. One trend is to consider proof of purchase to be the title page of a manual. (I've seen one title page become a "pass-along" treasure among users, especially with competitive upgrades.) Title pages do not provide enough protection to the software provider. I like an original diskette as proof of purchase.

- Make sure your product includes enough added value to discourage customers from stealing your software. This can be accomplished with reasonable pricing, superb documentation, and reference guides that cannot easily be copied, or by sending newsletters to registered customers or providing excellent phone support. Be creative in encouraging users to purchase their own software.

  If a customer can download your application from a BBS and buy a "self help" guide that is better written than your original manual (usually for less than $30), you are potentially giving away your product. The trend of delivering applications software on CD ROM can dramatically reduce the temptation for illegal duplication.

How Often Should You Upgrade Your Product?

Do you release software upgrades frequently enough? Most major software products tend to be updated on a once-per-18-month cycle. For those products that are updated less frequently, the temptation is strong for customers to switch to competitive products that release updates more frequently.

On the other hand, updating a product too frequently can strain your relationship with customers, for these reasons:

Training and installation costs. This is a major problem for large corporations who potentially need to train and install software for hundreds or even thousands of users for each upgrade.

Cost. "I thought we just *paid* for an upgrade?"

Perception. If the releases are not substantial enhancements over previous versions, you could get viewed as a company that "milks customers."

Although there is no rule of thumb for determining an update cycle, updating software every 9 to 15 months is rapidly becoming an industry norm. This update schedule appears to satisfy customers' desire for updates that are neither too frequent nor too infrequent. As I've previously mentioned, your marketing group needs to start planning for the next version early, preferably before the previous version ships.

Keeping Up with State-of-the-Art Technology

Software Engineering—Portability

This is a tough one. Do you create products that are "best-of-breed" on a given platform or do you create "not-so-best-of-breed" products that are independent of the platform? By platform, I am referring to Windows, DOS, and UNIX. You don't want to build products that can work both in DOS and UNIX environments when your customer base can only afford low-cost PCs. There is no competitive advantage in developing products on platforms with little to no customer purchasing interest. In fact, you could build products that are "killers" on a single platform and reap substantial profits as long as that platform remains predominant for your customer base.

Certainly, Microsoft is not suffering by building best-of-breed applications for Windows and Windows/NT.

But what if the industry changes? (And it *will* change.) Microsoft may currently own the largest market share of word processing applications for Windows, but WordPerfect provides a compelling suite of compatible solutions for a number of platforms including DOS, UNIX, OS/2, and Windows.

Building platform-independent applications is difficult. In turn, retrofitting applications designed for one platform onto another platform is extremely difficult. The implementation platform you choose should depend on your company's market opportunities—*not* on which platform (or platform development tools) you prefer.

I am in awe of companies that can develop platform-independent "killer" applications. Two good examples are Frame Technology and USData (my company).

Your Language of Choice

With the proliferation and widespread interest in computer language tools, it's important to keep in mind that, although some languages (like BASIC) are easy to use, performance and other key factors may severely limit the future of your products.

Languages that encourage a "hacking" mentality (experiment as you go) are outstanding for building utilities or customized solutions for specific customers. But sharing of source code with more than one developer can become a nightmare if the language environment provides little enforcement of modularization and structure.

For most developers, C has been the language of choice for years. As wonderful as C is, its low-level nature tends to give it the appearance of "assembly language with style." However, the paradigm used to construct data objects with member functions is so compelling with C++ that I have endorsed C++ as the best language that is powerful enough to build complex products.

How can C++ benefit your organization? Let me count the ways with a brief review of some key features of the language:

1. **Objects.** Modules that contain data as well as programmatic functions that use the data. These objects can be reused and interchanged with other software components.
2. **Polymorphism.** The ability for an object to invoke other objects without knowing the object's specific characteristics.
3. **Encapsulation.** Hiding the internal behavior of an object so that the external interfaces (data and object member functions) are the only interfaces visible.
4. **Inheritance.** The ability for objects to inherit properties from other objects.

Some of your developers might resist moving to C++ but, in my opinion, they have no valid reason for holding that view. At a minimum, insist that your developers place a C++ API around a set of C libraries already in use. Then, gradually migrate your engineers to take advantage of more advanced C++ features. C++ will reinforce good software engineering habits if your C++ objects are properly designed.

What about compilers? Again, the right choice depends on your goals. If your goal is to develop applications for a specific operating system platform, then by all means choose the best tool for that platform. You really can't go wrong with Microsoft C++ if you're developing applications for Windows or Windows NT.

However, if you wish to use the best C++ on a variety of platforms (such as OS/2, Windows, DOS, and Windows NT), I've found that the best provider is Borland. Their debugging environment, code generation, and reliability (here let me spell it: R•E•L•I•A•B•I•L•I•T•Y) is superb. Borland's customer support is also good.

One suggestion that I have for all compiler vendors is to provide more network-independent debugging! Since many developers use networks other than Novell (such as IBM's Token Ring, Artisoft's Lantastic, and Microsoft's Windows for Workgroups), allow debugging sessions to be distributed where one PC is debugging another. Most networks support NetBIOS interaction, yet most compiler's network debugging capabilities are limited to specific networks such as Novell's SPX/IPX. The network session requirements for remote debugging are minimal, so I don't understand why the compiler vendors don't "wise up." I hope they will.

Documenting Software Modules

Although it is important to keep specifications updated, unless your engineers are heavily motivated (or threatened) they need to be encouraged to keep technical specifications up to date. One method is to embed specifications in the source code as comments. There would be a great business opportunity if someone could write an extractor that would create a beautiful, well-formatted spec from a source document file!

Building Products that Are Field Customizable

I've already explained the importance of developing products that fit your particular customer base. However, some customers may require custom features, such as:

- Custom menu options
- Extensions to features already provided
- Integration with another application (either custom or off-the-shelf)
- Import and export to standard files formats
- Command automation (no "keyboard stuffing," please)

If your organization has to respond to each custom request, you'll be swamped. Why not design a product that allows for a field-based software engineering group to customize your applications and make money at it, too?

Let me elaborate on some interesting approaches that solve custom requests.

- **Custom menu options.** Provide a resource file that has definitions of each menu so that the definitions can be modified without changing any source code. Or, better yet, provide a text file that specifies each menu option and an associated action (or verb) that is dynamically loaded when you start your application.

- **Extensions to features already provided.** Provide an API that can be used by other software to "drive" the operation of your application. Or, design an API set of "hooks" so that your software can be called back at the point of every major operation. ROM-based process control systems frequently use this technique to hook out to a bank of RAM-defined entry points (preluded with simple RETurns) to support customer change requests or bugs. Windows applications can typically provide this same technique with dynamic-link libraries (DLL), which can be updated without releasing the entire software application.

- **Integration with another application (either custom or off-the-shelf).** With such Windows capabilities as the clipboard, DDE (dynamic data exchange), and OLE (object linking and embedding), you can employ numerous techniques for integrating your application with other applications. The beauty of this approach is that, as long as you follow the proper integration protocols and formats, you can pass your information to other software products that are better suited to analysis (such as spreadsheets, presentation graphics packages, or even word processors).

- **Import and export to standard files formats.** If it makes sense for your application, take advantage of the opportunity to support standard import and export formats: WMF, BMP, WK1, XLS, RTF, TIFF, PCX, and so on.

  Don't reinvent the code to handle these formats; there are tons of third-party libraries that can take care of format conversions for you. Place your internal resources on your application's added value—not on technologies that you can readily purchase.

- **Command automation.** Many applications should be able to operate unattended, so that batch operations can be run overnight. One technique is to record keystrokes using macro techniques. These captured keystrokes can then be replayed at a later time.

  The problem with this technique is that "keystroke stuffing" (well, that's what I call it) during macro playback requires the same environment that existed when the keystrokes were originally recorded. If some unexplained error condition occurs, the keyboard-stuffing technique will probably fail.

Figure 8.1 Building products that can be field customized

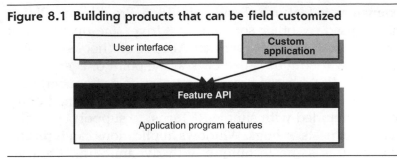

Instead, you may wish to consider designing your application so that its complete functionality is exposed as either a scripting or as a programming interface, as shown in Figure 8.1.

A scripting language could be fed into a custom application in a way that controls the application operation. Even though the application's user interface may change (it often does from version to version), custom applications should not be affected. An example of this technique is implemented in the WordBASIC command language, which has been historically used in Microsoft Word for Windows.

This technique serves two purposes: It provides for batch operation and a framework for customized applications (by using your base application almost like an "engine"). This concept is very powerful—all it takes is some forethought when the product is being designed. Retrofitting an application that was not originally designed for customization can be very difficult (if not impossible).

Building Global Products

Software companies are finding that, in many cases, their highest growth markets exist outside of the United States. Except for some areas in the Far East, the English language that we take for granted is not used. In addition, the semantics associated with software designed for an American customer may not work properly for, say, the British market.

Several examples quickly come to mind:

- Filtering alphabetics correctly
- Mandatory value-added tax (VAT)
- Currency formats

- Dates
- Terminology that is unfamiliar to other cultures or business environments
- Spelling ("color" vs. "colour")

As U.S. companies become more global, their software should be designed with enough flexibility to accommodate global customer needs. The same fact holds true for developers in other countries. I know of no reference that can help here, other than polling key representatives from around the world who can offer advice during a product's early design.

The few experts in the United States who have successfully developed worldwide applications software are worth their weight in gold. You may pay a big price for this kind of talent, but their experience is hard to come by. Perhaps the best and most economical solution (if you want or need to develop software for global use) is to hire experienced developers from foreign countries even if only on a temporary basis.

Application Frameworks

This is one of my favorite topics. The use of an application framework can dramatically reduce the effort (and, of course, time to market) required to build an application. An application framework is typically a set of run-time libraries that support many features that you, as a software engineer, would otherwise have to build "from scratch." The best application frameworks are those that provide both a well-defined API for your application and a visual method of creating your application.

You must decide whether you wish to build products on a given operating system platform or if you wish to build products that are less dependent on a given platform. A number these frameworks can currently produce highly efficient code, yet are easy to construct.

Regardless of the specific approach you choose, focus your energies on your application's added value and use off-the-shelf frameworks that will help you get to market faster. What should you look for in a good application framework?

- Stability of the vendor and a reputation, supported by your software engineers, that the product is reliable.

- Customer support that is technical enough to support you when you ask those difficult programming questions.
- No-cost run-time licenses for use of portions of the application framework. Keeping track of customer licenses and royalties can be very cumbersome. Of course, if the framework you want to use requires some form of royalty, you may have no choice. But shop around first. There are many competitive offerings that do not require royalties.

Before I leave the topic of operating system platform independence, I should mention that you can typically produce better applications by using a framework designed for a single platform (such as Windows). The use of an ill-designed framework (which often is so-called "platform independent) can frequently result in applications that don't particularly look or behave well on any platform!

There is at least one exception to this phenomenon: Inmark Development Corporation's fabulous zApp C++ framework. Inmark's zApp was developed from technology used in their existing applications, which had to execute on a variety of platforms. So, Inmark was already well equipped to address issues of "platform-independence" that were first raised years ago. With the proliferation of C++ compilers and their language benefits becoming so predominant, zApp's class libraries form an outstanding foundation for generic application building. And zApp uses the same API for other platforms, such as DOS and OS/2. Wow!

Client/Surfer

In one of my presentations, I discussed the pressing need for our organization to "provide Client/Surfer solutions." I couldn't understand why the California attendees were laughing uncontrollably while people from the East Coast were just staring in disbelief.

Obviously, I need to work on my pronunciation.

Anyway, with the down scaling of minicomputers and mainframes to server technologies located on LANs, we have at our fingertips the opportunity to exploit:

- **Distributed file and database systems**. Although a LAN once provided a great way to share printer and file information, the fact that multiple servers can now house database systems that are fully distributed could actually reshape the way we provide accessible information to a wide variety of connected applications (running on, of course, PCs).

- **Work flow**. Along with distributed file and database systems has come the use of remote programs (normally called "agents") that make sure files and database objects are actually routed between servers and, ultimately, users. Activities that can take place in the background while more effective electronic mail APIs (for example) are implemented in the foreground will absolutely revolutionize corporations that use networks more to deliver information than to support remote file and printer facilities.

- **Distributed execution.** The agents I've mentioned can provide tremendous benefits to a networked environment, where huge amounts of database searching or computation-intensive operations can be best executed remotely. The upcoming distributed computing environment (DCE) standards should yield a consistent programmatic interface that will allow servers to provide service on almost any imaginable platform (UNIX, OS/2, Windows NT, and so on).

Documentation

If you've never written a software user's manual, you have no idea how difficult it is to construct documentation while an application is being developed. If, during the development cycle, the application's flow and user interface is a moving target, the writers find it nearly impossible to keep up with the task of providing accurate documentation.

This phenomenon is typically not appreciated by anyone outside of documentation. But it must be recognized by you, the leader. Why you? You should be able to leave documentation issues to the writers, right?

Wrong.

Without your support, discipline regarding documentation will be thrown out the window by engineering and marketing to get the best product out to the customer base. Ever heard comments like these?

"If we can't adjust the application as we go, how can we take advantage of what we learn? I won't be told how to manage my project by a bunch of writers!" The results of this management philosophy (which isn't really management at all) have the same engineering (or marketing) manager saying, "Well we've got the software ready to go and we're waiting on the documentation. They say it will take another five weeks to finish up and get the manuals through production. This is *totally unacceptable!*"

"Totally unacceptable" is a favorite phrase of frustrated managers.

I've yet to hold up a project simply to wait for documentation to be completed. (Well, maybe one week at the most due to a printer production problem.) I don't have to, because I make sure the basic product flow and user interface are established at the start of each project.

If the team does not arbitrarily change the product after an early experimentation stage, unnecessary documentation-related delays will not take place. Getting the application's flow and user interface "buttoned down" by the alpha milestone not only reduces risk in achieving your ultimate ship date, but also helps to ensure that you have accurate documentation ready to go at or prior to your release date.

A customer satisfaction problem can present itself if documentation is not accurate. I've read README.TXT (alias "release notes") files that are almost as large as the user's manual. What's worse, and I *still* don't believe this one, one manual was accompanied by a separate sheet of paper—with references to page numbers full of documentation errors. In this one manual, several of the screen shots were even unintelligible! Apparently, nobody had proofread the manual's final "blue lines" (pre-production paper masters). As far as I was concerned, that product was a loser. The software vendor obviously was not in control and didn't demonstrate a desire for customer satisfaction in its product.

So, for you folks not directly responsible for documentation, be patient and plan for the need to do the right thing (pronounced "thang" in Texas). There are few feelings in development more satisfying than the one that occurs when you know you're ready to deliver software to production *with* accurate, beautiful manuals—ready to be inserted in the shipping containers!

Choosing the Right Tools

To provide best-of-breed documentation, you certainly need the right tools. These normally include the following:

- Desktop publisher
- Grammar and spelling checker
- Screen capture utility
- Drawing program

The number of available products in all of these areas makes it difficult to choose "the best." In fact, I own *all* of them. Each product has its strengths and weaknesses, so I'm not going to spend time evaluating them for you. Besides, your documentation needs may be dramatically different from mine.

Your documentation group must align itself with marketing goals in order to prioritize the style of documentation that is the most critical for your customers.

- Is color important to your customers? Spot color will generally work just fine for headers and/or footers and tints.
- Are sideheads important? Sideheads are text placed in the margins for emphasis. If you use sideheads, your software must allow you to work with side by side text so that sideheads move in tandem with associated normal text; otherwise managing sideheads manually will drive your writers crazy.
- Do you use tables extensively? Table generation, if done repetitively, needs some sort of style automation.
- Do you need automatic table and figure captions? Tracking automatic figure and table numbering is very difficult if done by hand.
- Is automatic drawing/image frame-sizing, with anchoring to text paragraphs, important? The placement of images that scroll along with text changes is a very powerful feature. In addition, if these images can be referenced by relative file naming (to a subdirectory, for example) rather than to a specific filename (where the subdirectories are explicit), you'll have more flexibility when you have multiple writers working on a single document.
- Is reliability and product performance critical? It had better be.

Using the above criteria as the basis for our company's needs, we investigated the leading desktop publishing products: Ventura Publisher, PageMaker, QuarkXPress, and FrameMaker. To compare our needs with your company's, I'm assuming that paragraph styles, table of contents, and index generation are mandatory desktop publishing features. A few warnings: If one of your requirements for documentation folks is ease-of-use, forget it. All, and I mean *all*, desktop publishers are difficult to learn; their ease-of-use is questionable.

Perhaps you have resigned yourself (because your writers want it this way) to do all of the documentation work in a word processor and then, for the final steps, you will convert the manuals into a desktop publisher. If you agree to this approach, you are frankly out of your mind. With the sophistication of present desktop publishers, it is just as easy to type in Ventura Publisher as it is to enter text in Word for Windows, as long as documentors are given the proper computer equipment to effectively use the desktop publishing software

And, by the way, word processors do provide a full range of writing tools that are not dramatically less functional than the modern-day desktop publisher. But without the extensions of color support, kerning, typographic controls, and other sophisticated controls, a word processor will produce less than professional publication results. In fact, I can always tell when a document was produced using a word processor in place of a desktop publisher. *Always.*

Based on our decision criteria, we quickly dropped QuarkXPress because it offered no integrated table of contents, indexing, or figure/table numbering capability. Extensions are available for accomplishing these tasks, but these additions are not cheap and are not part of the base product.

We did not choose PageMaker. Although a superb product, PageMaker's inability to support table/figure numbering and sideheads couldn't match what our documentation needed to communicate. If we had adjusted our requirements, PageMaker would have definitely been chosen.

Now we come to the showdown: Ventura Publisher versus FrameMaker. In terms of feature comparisons, there is relatively little difference between these two outstanding products. When the criteria present identical (or near identical) results, what do you do? Being a longtime Ventura Publisher shop, we examined the problems that we had previously faced using Ventura Publisher. Sure enough, FrameMaker seemed to handle some of these problems successfully. Customer support at Ventura was not, in our opinion, up to par. And reliability was always a problem since we had not upgraded to newer versions in the past two years. Why should we? The Windows version had not really advanced beyond the user interface design that was in use since the earliest GEM implementations. People who have not seen the recent advances in user interface design have their head in the sand.

FrameMaker satisfied our basic criteria and was even able to provide compatible solutions on a variety of platforms (such as Windows NT, UNIX, and Mac).

I haven't regretted the move to FrameMaker but with Ventura's migration under Corel's leadership I expect great things.

Now I need to address the issue of drawing packages. Why not use the drawing tool that is bundled with the desktop publisher you've purchased? There is a good reason not to. Some of your diagrams may need to be integrated with collateral material and, if your advertising group uses a different desktop publisher tool, the drawings that you develop for manuals may have to be completely redone using other tools. If you work smart at the start, you'll save the company money every time!

This explains why screen shots are being made, with outstanding results, using such products such as Window Painters' SnapPRO! or the exceptional U-Lead's ImagePals, and drawings are often being done using Shapeware's ViSiO.

Going On-line

One of the most heated controversies among documentation folks revolves around the issue of on-line documentation. Should you put documentation on-line? Most customers say, "That would be great!" And as soon as you acquiesce, you'll probably hear, "Hey, your on-line documentation took up 10 megabytes on my disk! What gives?"

More and more companies are putting documentation on-line and reducing the size of their manuals. Of course, it's always possible to place manuals on a CD ROM. However, inserting, initializing, and reading a CD ROM disk simply to gain access to a manual may be too cumbersome to a customer. If you decide to augment your documentation with extensive training or multimedia enhancements, the use of CD ROM is perfect. If the user wishes to print the documentation (or a subset of it), please offer that capability.

PC configurations are offering CD ROM players now as standard equipment (remind you of a tape deck in cars?). So, if at all possible, take advantage of this medium. The cost to produce CDs is not high and actually offers a form of copy protection. Why? Because, unlike diskettes, the average corporate user cannot afford CD mastering equipment or even a CD player.

Getting Customers to Return Registration Cards

You might be tempted to entice your customers to fill in their registration card by providing a reward (for instance another reference manual—or something similar). This only begs the question, "Why didn't they include the manual when I bought the product?" This reward is actually an additional inconvenience. Never try to give the customer something for their registration effort that they should have originally received.

What Level of Documentation Is Really Necessary?

I frequently hear that customers "never use the manual." I think it must be a macho thing to expect good software to be completely self-documenting. That's certainly an ideal situation, but even so, there are circumstances where a manual is great to have "in case of emergencies."

It is not unusual for the level of documentation required to be dictated by some predefined page count. This has always been a mystery to me since the page count is dependent on the complexity of the application, amount of white space used in the manual, font sizes, number of diagrams and screen shots, and other factors. Regulating the quality of the manual to fit some preconceived page count criterion is short sighted, and the results could adversely affect customer satisfaction.

Marketing and documentation should originally agree on the intended customer base for the documentation. Having accomplished this, you should let the documentation manager do the right thing. If the intended customer base is highly technical,

then chances are a reference manual with
may be required. If the intended customer bas
end users with little to no technical background,
to explain each feature in great detail. In this situat
ing end users with a detailed reference manual that
the technical theory behind the application will miss the

Documentation, when targeted correctly, has another s
prising benefit. Some potential customers will actually make
their purchase decision after viewing the documentation. Have
you ever considered purchasing software and, by thumbing
through the manual, realized that the documentation is incom-
prehensible? I have.

I've even express-mailed our documentation set to customers who expressed a desire to purchase a large amount of software. In three cases that I can remember, the customer purchased
the software because they were impressed with our documentation. (By the way, they also liked the software.)

Quality Assurance

To round out the development disciplines, I wanted to save the
best for last. The folks responsible for testing your products
deserve a lot of respect.

Automated Testing Basics

If you currently test your software using "power users," you
are surely out of date. I haven't tested that way in more than
seven years. And for good reason:

- **Automated tests save time.** Since human testing is very labor
  intensive, the time required to execute tests depends on the
  number of testers you are using. In case you haven't already
  heard this fact, computers can execute tests at speeds millions
  of times faster than any human can type. You simply can't
  afford to *not* use automated test techniques.

- **Automated tests save money.** True, you will need to purchase another computer to execute automated tests, and test
  creation can be time consuming. But once you have created
  the test environment and the associated test scripts, the cost

tests in place of hiring profes-
...l.

...**urate.** When you manually test com-
...less you follow a test plan to the letter,
...an error during the test is as probable as
...in the application. The ability to record test
...y important because it should be possible to re-
...scripts to recreate problems.

...nated tests can cover a higher percentage of code paths.
...plication software has thousands upon thousands of possible paths to take. Designing test scripts that can traverse
through as many combinations as possible will undoubtedly
improve the confidence of the test coverage.

- **Automated tests can actually drive problem-tracking automation.** One of the most exciting opportunities in testing technology is the integration of automatic testing with bug-tracking
  software management systems. Let me explain. If you implement a bug-tracking system that can track a programmer's
  ownership of specific software modules, you are leaps and
  bounds ahead of most software developers.

  If you work on a network where all of your team members
  are connected, and you use a sophisticated electronic mail
  system, you are in great shape. It's possible for automated
  test software to log an error, check which module (or sub-
  system) the error occurred in, and retrieve the name of the
  programmer associated with the problem. The software would
  then save the test script that caused the problem and, finally,
  would send an electronic mail message to the programmer
  (along with the test script) informing the programmer that an
  error occurred. And, of course, you'll know when the engineer received the notification because the mail message sets
  the status for "reply notification" (or certified return). Wow.

Beta Testers

It's an industry-wide standard to use key customers to test
products prior to their release. And that makes sense. Customers will use your application software in ways that you couldn't
have imagined. As a normal course of doing business, it is well
worth the effort to use beta testers.

But why is it an effort? Well, marketing needs to choose beta customers that will really use the product as you expect. And your customer support organization must be trained on the product in order to provide support to these beta customers. If beta customers have nobody to communicate with, they will quickly get discouraged and stop testing the software. It is always a good idea to have a special phone number available (through CompuServe or bulletin board) along with other electronic means for contacting customer support. And by all means, reward your best beta customers with a finished copy of the application!

You must allocate enough time for beta testing. Your beta customers really need time to use it effectively. A beta period less than one month is just too short.

How do you handle beta customer feature feedback? At this point in the development cycle, any major feature requests should be postponed to the next release. Marketing must set the proper expectations with beta customers so that they realize feature requests cannot be handled at this late date.

Do not expect your beta customers to find problems that your quality assurance organization doesn't have to find. I can't tell you how often I've heard this excuse: "Our beta customers didn't find the problem." Don't accept that. Beta testing is just icing on the cake. Your QA people are responsible for *baking* the cake. And icing on a lousy cake can't mask the basic taste: lousy.

Customer Support

Although this book does not do justice to the topic of customer support (we would have to write another book), a couple of relationships deserve to be explored.

Relationship with Documentation

Ever considered holding your technical publications (documentation) group accountable for the issues that customer support raises? By "accountable" I mean that your documentation manager's performance is partly based on the "pain threshold" felt by customer support.

This approach really works. I have always assumed that, if a product's documentation is effective, customers will find the correct information before calling customer support. As mentioned earlier, we once tracked the majority of customer support calls to the installation of our application software. For the next version of our software, we revamped the Installation Guide; customer support had virtually no calls concerning installation. A successful recovery!

Relationship to the Whole Development Process

Any size company (I mean *any* size company) should be able to tie together the following activities using networks and new application software:

- **Trouble report.** Incoming trouble calls should be assigned a customer incident number.

- **Bug database.** Since quality assurance normally keeps track of problems in a product, customer support should be able to link their trouble report incident to a given bug. When a bug is fixed, the customer support representatives could get notified automatically in order to respond to those customers that are waiting specifically for that problem to be corrected.

- **Fax transmission.** Customer support representatives should be able to fax a response directly from their PC to a centralized fax server system. Also, customers should be able to dial into a fax system and choose a document to fax back.

- **CompuServe or bulletin board.** Last, but not least, providing a public forum for bugs, sales, and other product information is becoming an important customer benefit.

Relationship with the Development Team

It's a big mistake not to use the customer support organization as a key contributor to the development team. Customer support has one of the best perspectives on your customers' expectations and frustrations. Doesn't it make sense to hear the customer support perspective when the application is being designed? In addition, customer support tends to develop a "sixth sense" about product usability.

If you don't properly take advantage of your internal resources, you'll pay for it later in customer satisfaction problems.

Getting Training

"Could you send me to this training class?"

Looking up from my desk, I see the sorriest face.

"I could be a better programmer if I could go to this class."

"How much is it?" I ask.

"Oh, I don't know—around $895" is the response.

"And where is it?"

"Well, we just missed the one here in Dallas. The next one is in Santa Monica."

"Santa Monica in California? You mean the resort right next to the beach?"

"Yeah, I guess so—I don't know much about it."

Ever had a conversation like that? Without training, though, your folks cannot keep up with the industry. Unfortunately, it seems as though the majority of training seminars provide no tangible results. With airfare, hotel, food, and transportation, the $895 training course easily becomes a $2,500 expenditure per person (not to mention time away from the office). Self-help videos are becoming real helpful and very inexpensive. For example, Borland's "World of C++" is exceptional!

In Summary

This has been a fun book to write. If you are a development manager, review the Rules for the Unruly, Reality Checks, and Practical Maniac Tips in Chapters 1 through 7. Then pass the book to your marketing manager, your finance officer, and your sales manager. The goal of this book is to provide a level of professionalism to a business that appears to have few rules and few incentives.

It's rare to receive compliments in this line of work; however, I received one from a quality assurance person who left our company to work in another part of the country. I thought it would be worth printing:

"I have a lot of respect for you. I've never met a person who could motivate such a diverse group of people and make them all feel proud of the job they're doing. And that's *before* all the food and booze!"

I hope this book helps you earn your share of compliments and, overall, to be successful in the challenging role as a manager and leader of development maniacs. (P.S. Don't forget one of your best motivators: all the food and booze.)

A Maniac's Glossary

The following terms are software maniac expressions that I've used in this book. If you're unsure about the meaning of any of these terms, these definitions should clarify things for you. You'll find some of these terms in the dictionary, but you won't find most of the following definitions there. When dealing with maniacs, you might as well throw out the dictionary.

Awesome   A statement of fact expressed whenever a major milestone has been achieved. If you use the term "awesome" too often and in other contexts, you should return quickly to the 1980s.

Buy-in   Getting everyone in your organization (or on a team) to participate in resolving one or more issues. You will have to play an initial role as a facilitator in order to listen to everyone's ideas; however, your role should change to that of a leader in order to make a decision. Everyone might not agree with your decision, but they should all feel that their opinions were heard and that reasons were presented to back up the final decision.

Circular reference   *See* Round-robin.

Closure   Getting a decision agreed upon quickly, with buy-in. If you don't get buy-in, you didn't get proper closure. *See* Buy-in.

Consensus   Letting everyone in your organization (or on a team) participate in resolving one or more issues—a decision is not made unless there is 100-percent agreement. *See also* Buy-in.

209

Cost of goods   The total cost of the materials and labor required to produce and ship the final product. Typically abbreviated as COGS.

Individual contributor   Development personnel that do not have management personnel.

Milestone   The formal point in a project where specific team-agreed requirements have all been satisfied.

Nerd herd   A friendly term used to describe developers.

Nuke   Instead of saying you have "terminated" someone or "deleted" a critical file, you should use this abbreviated form of "nucleated." It strikes fear throughout a development organization and disbelief outside of development. Use sparingly for maximum impact. If marketing starts using "nuke," find another term. "Nuke" must only be used by developers.

Politics   Although the term has many meanings, you engage in this addictive habit any time you undermine fellow employees in a negative way—that is—"behind their backs." Politics is addictive because it is an easy habit to develop and a very difficult one to shake.*

Prima donna-ism   So full of yourself and your talents that you become too difficult to manage or lead.

Product manager   The position in marketing that has overall responsibility for the definition, revenues, and overall success of a given product.

Project manager   Typically the engineering manager that is responsible, as a partner to the product manager, for the development of a given product.

Problem categories   The types of problems that customer support tracks. Examples include installation and reports.

---

*Developers tend to be lousy at playing politics—they're too obvious when they try it. On the other hand, marketing and sales tend to thrive on playing this game. Where ego and visibility are important to your department or your company, politics tends to spread like a virus unless management stops it quickly whenever it makes its presence known. Don't let it spread!

Round-robin *See* Circular reference.

Sandbagging A term normally used to describe schedules that are so "padded" that the team is guaranteed to deliver by that date. Never use this term (especially with marketing); instead, use terms like "realistic" or "planning for the eventual problems and unknown situations."

SFAS-86 The Statement of Financial Accounting Standards (SFAS) number 86, which requires some development expenses to be capitalized once technical feasibility has been achieved.

Team Includes individuals who have equal participation in developing a project. Equal "participation" does not mean "decisions by consensus," but that decisions will include participation by all team members. In development, the team includes engineering, quality assurance, and documentation.

Yappin' Used to distinguish someone as a brilliant talker but not necessarily a good listener. If you consistently do the most yappin' then you're probably buffaloin' your audience rather than offering them an opportunity to contribute.

Index

213